THE REAL FRIDAY JONES
A Self-Help Memoir

THE REAL FRIDAY JONES
A Self-Help Memoir

Written by

Khansa Jones-Muhammad,
"The Real Friday Jones"

Friday Jones Publishing
Culver City, California

The Real Friday Jones
Published by
Friday Jones Publishing
PO Box 329
Culver City, CA 90232
310-508-3248
therealfridayjones@gmail.com

Friday Jones, Publisher / Editorial Director
Yvonne Rose/Qualitypress.info, Book Packager

ALL RIGHTS RESERVED

No part of this book may be reproduced or transmitted in any form or by any means—electronic or mechanical, including photocopying, recording or by any information storage and retrieval system—without written permission from the authors, except for the inclusion of brief quotations in a review.

Friday Jones Books are available at special discounts for bulk purchases, sales promotions, fund raising or educational purposes.

Copyright © 2017 by Khansa Jones-Muhammad
ISBN #: 978-1-9372696-0-9
Library of Congress Control #: 2016960414

DEDICATION

Fric & Frac a mother's love knows no boundaries

Anafghat Ayouba of Niamey, Niger

Amina Lawal of Katsina, Nigeria

The Children Born into Brothels, India

The Child Slaves of India's Rock Quarries

Girls Everywhere

I see pieces of me in you.

ACKNOWLEDGEMENTS

To my therapist, I could not have gone through this process without you. My perception of your work has been that it is your legacy. Mental health and emotional well-being can be so overlooked in American Society. I appreciate your facilitating my journey to find my whole self.

Salaams Bro – God gives us family, and we have the luxury of choosing friends. I am oh so blessed that Mother Father God sent you to be a living angel to watch over me. I love you.

PJ hopefully through this lens you can see me and find understanding in my path and appreciate how different it is from yours. I truly adore you more than you know.

R. Chang, my thinking friend. These words inspired me so that I had to share them: "I love your writing. I'm not a fan of the world but you make me think. My instinct is to tell you to close ranks. Closing ranks is out of fear and hatred of a thoughtless world. Then I read your thoughts and I think about the good people out there. The writers who share their lives so that we don't feel isolated even in our clicks. So, write on (right-on). Keep doing you and maybe I won't worry about doing me." That is the point of it all. Thank you for your friendship.

Yvonne and Tony Rose - I started this journey with you not knowing the landscape. I thank you for your guidance, your patience, and your encouragement. The telling of this story would not have happened without you both and I appreciate you!

CONTENTS

INTRODUCTION: Hello World..1

THE ROAD TO SELF-DISCOVERY BEGINS........................3

    Part 1: My Mom...5

    Part 2: Me..8

    Part 3: The College BF..14

    Part 4: The Porn Star..21

    Part 5: The Actor..26

    Part 6: Little Friday..31

THE ISSUES...35

    Part 1: Articulate What You Most Love About You............37

    Part 2: The Fear of Telling...44

    Part 3: The Therapist Dissects Me.......................................52

    Part 4: Understanding Your Self-Concept...........................57

    Part 5: Running from Hostile Environments.......................63

    Part 6: Release Your Primary Experiences..........................70

    Part 7: A Soul and Spirit Unsettled......................................75

    Part 8: The Forgiveness Letter...81

THE ROAD TO FORGIVENESS...89

    Part 1: The Contemplation...91

    Part 2: Forgiving an Outlier...96

    Part 3: A Key to Life..101

Part 4: The Virginians..104
Part 5 When It's Important...109
Part 6: Mean People..111
Part 7: Knucklehead Relations..115
Part 8: Acceptance..119

REBUILDING A NEW YOU...125
Part 1: Accounting..127
Part 2: Practice..132
Part 3: The Final Chapter...139

ABOUT THE AUTHOR..147

INTRODUCTION

HELLO WORLD!

Posted on July 20, 2012

This is my first Blog…. Why did I start Blogging? Therapy. I have a life that has had bumps, bruises, and scars in a couple of places. As I strive to develop my true voice, I aspire to get in touch with the inner child that experienced a loss of innocence at the ripe age of six years old. I am starting this blog to document some of my life experiences and say all of the *ish* I want to say in an unapologetic way – kind of like Lil Wayne.

If you are not a Lil Wayne fan, here is the lowdown: his second or third album flopped and he had a host of written material. In order to free himself, from what he felt was holding him back, he went into an epic recording session that lasted days where he recorded every lyric he had ever written until that time. Since that session, Lil Wayne has been a freestyle rapper and has consistently sold hits. Now back to me for a second, the parallel is, I want to say and do all of the things I wanted to do when I was a child, experience life in a fully engaged and self-actualizing kind of way – so like Ludacris I can get the F out of my way – and live a freestyle life that is winning.

Rather than sit my mother down and hurt her feelings with family therapy, or sit face to face with the uncle that attempted to rape me as a child, or sitting and telling a therapist I regret never taking dance lessons when I really wanted to be a choreographer – me and my 40 year old self are going to tell it all to the world; in tandem with my therapy sessions that involve me and my therapist only, I am going to take dance and surf lessons NOW and Give opinions on things that I hope tickle you in some way. At some point, I will upgrade my website: www.TheRealFridayJones.com . I hope to have more followers, meet interesting people on my journey, get to my real life's purpose, inspire folks along the way, and say *ish* in an unapologetic kind of way. Ya heard!

And for the record – I am a black woman, and yes, we do go to therapy!

Unapologetically,

Friday

PS Follow me on Twitter@FridayJones1

THE ROAD TO SELF-DISCOVERY BEGINS

The summer heat sweltered, sweat began to bead on her forehead. Then she inhaled and took her first step.

The Real Friday Jones

PART 1

MY MOM

Posted on July 22, 2012

I first want to acknowledge Tony Clomax for the theme of this blog. He has an amazing web series called "The Twelve Steps to Recovery" that is about a lovable guy that was dumped by his girlfriend and left heartbroken. The main character's two best friends decide he needs to "recover" and set him up on 12 blind dates that lead to hilarious escapades.

Okay, now back to me. So my first assignment was to read an article explaining "The Language of Feelings" by David Viscott, MD. I believe he has written a host of books. The premise is: Anxiety is the fear of Hurt or Loss. Hurt or Loss lead to Anger. Anger held in, leads to guilt. Guilt unrelieved, leads to depression. Then I had to think about how I have related emotionally in all of my past relationships. Work included – especially when things don't go well – and journal my insights. Yikes – here we go.

So before I started journaling, I made a wonderful Kamikaze from "Summer Cocktails and Other Refreshing Drinks." 1oz fresh lime juice, 1oz Cintreau or Triple Sec, 1oz Vodka, and a handful of ice.

Although this task was to include work relationships – I focused on more intimate relationships. The five people that came to mind were my mother, my college boyfriend, the porn star, my current love, and me. Respectively, my first love, the person I first fell in love with, the person I had potential to fall for, the person I am in love with, and the person I am learning to love. Ironically all of the fellows seemed to have another woman, another contender that seemed to form a triangle with me.

In an effort not to make each posting pages upon pages of reading, I will have to give this to you in pieces. So let's start with my mom. I could use another Kamikaze, but I digress, we are not forming poor habits during this process.

My mom sent my brother and me away for what was supposed to be a summer, to our grandfather's house in Virginia. That turned into what felt like an entire year – it may not have been; but I remember school starting and my mother was not there and my grandfather was not too happy about it. This was a time where there was a lot of loss, lack of control, lack of love, lack of self-esteem. My mom was gone. When she did come to Virginia, things were better, but our circumstances were not good; and frankly, the happiness and joy that I felt in growing up in Brooklyn, and knowing where I belonged, and living in a neighborhood that was familiar where everyone knew me, my mom and my grandmother were also lost to this new environment, with less than happy conditions.

We were on welfare, I had holes in my shoes, I am sure my brother did too – we were poor, and we knew it. As a child and teen, disappointing my mom was a constant concern. It's weird. I was smart, and my mother took great care in grooming my hair and making nice clothes for us; but even now although she has learned to keep her commentary to herself, I could be feeling great, then she would say you could use a better .... and just like that I was deflated, when I did not ask for an opinion.

I do not have a lot of memories of my mother telling me I was pretty or looked nice – I think she did her best to make sure I looked my best – but she did not tell me. She also never said things like 'you can trust me, you could never disappoint me' – and if she did, between the moves, the violence, the poverty and all of the disorder – I may have simply missed it. I do remember being told on the day I ran away from home in my favorite dress with my best friend, that there was good reason to not like the man she was choosing to marry. Her scare tactics, as learned from her mom, were things she said like "if you don't like it you can find somewhere else to live, or if you come home pregnant I will kick you out" – all of which was counterproductive, indicated I was not good enough, and kept a child that should have been verbal about what she was feeling, to just not talk about feelings, and left me to make poor choices. Not having a voice with a lot of things with my mom sucked – there was no feeling of safety with her; yet I would have been devastated to lose her or her love.

Unapologetically,

Friday

PART 2

ME

Posted on July 23, 2012

Yesterday I enjoyed a Kamikaze before delving into thoughts on my mom – no one really enjoys having difficult conversations about their parents, I am no exception. Today is more of a spa recovery day so I am going to enjoy one of my personal favorites – and you can tell it's one of my originals, because there are no true measurements – Mint infused lime water. Small bundle of mint leaves, 3 drops liquid trace minerals, 1/4 wedge of lime squeezed, 8oz water and ice. Right now, it's summer time, so most things will require a little ice.

Before talking about my loves…. Let's talk a little about me. Now, the assignment required that I focus on relationships that did not particularly go well. People do not frequently have conversations with themselves to make sure that their relationship with themselves is good. Are you compromising yourself to be with so and so, do you surround yourself with friends that build you up or break you down, do you even like yourself when you look in the mirror… do you occasionally look yourself in the eyes and smile and say hey I love you?

Now overall, I would say I have a good relationship with myself; but my internal dialogue sometimes can have its own agenda and move so fast, that my emotions wind up taking a real beating; and I am left standing there feeling like I have been on an emotional roller coaster. Sometimes it's hormonal and on that 28-day cycle, or sometimes it is circumstances that are not what I want them to be. I love me some me – but the inner child, well, she has had some challenges.

As a child there was a loss of something called innocence, that loss was a lack of control, being a kid, being a girl at the mercy of my crazy stepfather. The only reason the man did not have sex with me is because I told him that my mother told me that the penis was not supposed to touch my vagina and he was not sticking that thing in me. At six years old, this grown man was waking me up in the middle of the night sometimes, or even during the day after school asking me to lay down so he could perform cunnilingus on me. When my clitoris was engorged, he would start jerking himself off because he knew my little body was aroused. I hated it when he came, the drops onto my stomach always felt cold and disgusting. He kept a stash of Playboy's between my mother's mattress and I guess looking at the pictures with me was his version of foreplay. At first, I really did not understand that something was wrong with his behavior. And then, there was the night that I thought he was going to kill everyone that was most important to me.

I do not even know what set him off – but it did not take much – our apartment at that time had a front and a back. The back is where the kitchen, my brother's room, my room, the hallway and the bathroom were. The front is where the living-room and my mother's room was. He dragged my first love into the front, I remember being in tears and the feeling of suspended terror. Pleading with insanity made no difference, I was so small I was able to crawl under a side table that matched the coffee table in the living room. That night I learned what black and blue on brown skin looked like. This violence included a long serrated knife and death threats, until he literally fell asleep. To this day I have never purchased a serrated steak knife or serrated cutting knife of any kind. It was one of the longest nights in my life and fear and silence became synonymous overnight and mortality and the idea of an unjust world were things now that I clearly understood. When he came to my bed after that night and said, "if you ever tell your mother I will kill her." I believed him. That started the beginning of learning how to mask my feelings, the beginning of not having a voice.

In Virginia I was a girl in a house of boys – there was always the touching and if you tell, I will tell your mother. Somehow disappointing my mother is not something I wanted to do – probably because I did not want her to leave again. And to help you understand touching, me, my brother, my uncle DA, and his cousin we were the kids in the house and we were all about the same age. There were five other aunts and uncles that were grown, and one uncle GA that was about 19. My mother did not grow up with these siblings. It did not seem to matter to anyone that I was the only young girl in the mix. If there were sleep-overs it would be 'oh put the kids all in the living room'. My uncle DA and his cousin, especially, were always trying to touch the V-jayjay. There was a day I was taking a bath upstairs, my uncle went across the street to get his friend, because he thought it would be fun to kick the bathroom door in to see if they could see my nakedness. And then there was the night of the attempted rape that my then teenage uncle swears to this day did not happen – me, you, and God know the truth, dude.

For whatever reason, all of the adults piled into my grandfather's green van and went somewhere. I remember asking where they were going and being told they were grown and going out. Me and this teenage uncle were left alone. I was supposed to take a shower and go to bed. Well I went into the downstairs bathroom to get in the shower, and before I could turn the water on, he opened the door, undressed me and told me to go into the den and lay down, he laid on top of me and started humping. I was stark naked, he was between my legs and I could feel his penis getting harder and harder. As I was laying there at now the ripe age of seven, I was praying to god, "please let somebody come home." I knew if no-one came, there would be no saving me. Thankfully just as swiftly as it had disappeared, my grandfather's van reappeared pulling into the driveway and the lights shined through the den window. My uncle shoved me into the bathroom, handed me my clothes, turned the water on and ran upstairs to his room. When my mom, aunts, uncles and grandfather walked in through the living room, my teenage punk-assed uncle ran out the front door. I never said a word because I already understood that bad things could simply happen to little girls. The little girl in me was so violated.

Years later when I found out that this same uncle was going to have a daughter – we were on a family reunion in Virginia. My grandfather came up with my step-grandma and one of my aunts and her kids. I broke down and told my mom about my stepfather and about my uncle. The idea of a child being born to this man was my breaking point – my own daughter was 3-months-old, and I felt a responsibility to protect my baby and the little one being born to my uncle. As I explained it to my grandfather with the full support of my brother, I told him "you have grandchildren that are in his space – today he has no relevance in my life. You can do what you want with what I am telling you, but I would not allow him around your female grandchildren." My grandfather said, "I am an old man now, why didn't you tell me then when I could have kicked his ass, what do you want me to do now?" I told him "you can do what you want to do." Needless to say things with that side of the family have been challenged since then, but I really do not care because that part of my childhood – the Virginia years were hard. As an adult I get to choose whose company I keep.

I wore glasses, was teased and called 4 eyes, I had a scar from heart surgery, and was flat footed, and my feet hurt as a child. Anyway my self-esteem was terrible for years – I often covered myself with big clothes. And let's not talk about Junior High School. I went to a magnet school, but smart boys are still horny toads, and playtime on the school yard pre Anita Hill involved a lot of bra snapping, and copping a feel of my ass in the name of tag. Being one of the first girls with breasts large enough to rest on the lunch table made life interesting, and brought on more sexual attention than I, of all people, wanted. It was not until high school that I started working in retail at one of the trendiest stores in the Village, that I developed my own perception of my beauty – and I could express that by dressing what I considered well, silk shirts, palazzo pants, name brands like "Kikit" and "Marithe Francois Girbaud" were my staples. It was through developing my own image that I started to find joy in my full-sized breasts and rounded hips. Being a girl was not easy!

Unapologetically,

Friday

PART 3

THE COLLEGE BF

Posted on July 24, 2012

The College Boyfriend – the first relationship where I seemed to matter. There was no rush to sex like a mad boar. But in terms of a relationship that did not go well, this surely qualifies. This was the first true heartbreak, the one that left me shattered into a thousand little pieces.

Remember my assignment was to think about how I related emotionally and to journal my insights. I remember the first time I saw him on campus. I did not even know his name. He was walking on Howard University's campus heading up the hill towards the School of Business, and I was walking downhill. He had on a bright orange 3/4 length draw string jacket – I remember because I had one just like it. Our eyes met and there were no words, just a respectful nod. The next semester he was sitting behind me in an accounting class. I never said more than hello and goodbye until the day he wound up in a study group with some of my close friends. By then I already knew he was smart.

He was Chinese and Black by way of Jamaica. He was one of the most handsome men I knew. There was a moment in the study group when we were all on the floor of my friend's room and he was looking at me and talking. I was laying on my stomach writing notes… I noticed the way he was looking at me and with my knees bent behind me and my feet touching, I pushed myself back on the wall until my legs were in a split like position; and he noticed. It was real subliminal, no one else was paying me any attention and he stopped talking for a split second and I knew I had his attention. I told my friends I thought he was cute, he told the same friends he thought I was cute, and they started hooking us up. We all passed the midterm we were studying for and I decided to host a celebration party. It poured rain, cats and dogs, I did not think anyone would come – but the party was just part of being "hooked up." My friends, bless their souls, came and they brought my new-found friend with them. Because of the rain, folks basically ate and ran, but he stayed. We laid in my living room, and at that time I lived off campus in a cute little row house on 5th and O Street, NW. We talked until the sun came up. I knew I liked him.

It did not take him very long after that "party" to ask me out. How could I say no? It seemed like we were fairly inseparable then. Between class, studying, and having my own off-campus spot. I was in a new world with this guy. Jodeci had just come out, and I remember running that CD into the ground. My three roommates lived upstairs, and I had a room downstairs with my own bathroom. When he came over, the rest of the world did not exist. He never rushed me to have sex, he repeatedly told me whenever you are ready. I remember a time where he said something like I want you to know you can trust me around you, let me be naked with you. I didn't even know what that meant. Any time I had been naked in the presence of a man, sex was involved – not with him. One day he asked me to look at him and mirror his movements, we were naked, he got on his knees and so did I; he moved his hands in different directions and I moved how he moved; and then he traced my body with his hands, without touching me and then we laid there and spooned. I had never experienced anything like that before.

I was so body conscious because of my childhood experiences. When I tried to hide, or cover my nakedness, he would say things like you are beautiful or your body is beautiful – do not be ashamed to be naked in front of me, I love to see you. I felt respected and safe with him. He was smart and nerdy and fine and soft spoken. He did things around my apartment without my asking, and he cared about my grades. I loved him with childlike innocence – it was pure and so unconditional. I felt like this man had unlocked my heart and it was indeed his. But then there were the negatives.

Howard University's female to male ratio was something like 11:1. And there were plenty of opportunities for this man to lay with the dogs. The chicks that knew we were a couple still wanted to fuck him so they could say that they had. And I would always know, because something as simple as "hello" became somehow different, and I could see the nuances as if they were big bold letters written in body language. And I would, within confession sessions – a safe conversation with no judgment and no consequences – ask him if he had screwed so and so, and he would tell me that he had. But for whatever reason, because he was honest, I did not really care about the different one night stands. I am not sure what the chicks thought of me, maybe they didn't think I knew, perhaps they thought their secret was a secret – but he would tell me everything. And then there was his on again off again girlfriend, that was initially introduced to me as his "friend." She was a dark-skinned Indian looking girl from the Bay Area. I thought I was prettier than she was, but she had the most beautiful hair, kind of like my sister's hair. And although I knew I could grow my hair long, it would never be that textured natural hair like hers. I found a reason to discount myself.

I remember the day I found out the true depth of their "friendship." I was on campus in the Blackburn Center by myself for whatever reason. I had on a pair of crème-colored Girbaud Bermuda shorts, a crème-colored fitted ribbed t-shirt and a pair of black Mary Jane shoes with a black belt. I had seen them talking in what looked like a heated discussion, and I guess she had had enough. I momentarily interrupted and he said I will meet you at Blackburn. Well she came to me. He asked her not to do this but she proceeded to tell me 'this brother is mine, he has told me he is seeing you, but I am telling you, I am going to keep seeing him and sleeping with him as long as I want to'. I was done (so I thought). I told him right there it was over, did my best to walk away composed, but I could not breathe – it was like I was hyperventilating; and as soon as I got outside the glass doors, and could breathe air, I broke down and started crying in broad daylight. None of my friends seemed to be on the yard that day; tears streamed down my face, as I cried out loud. She was the one girl that he did not tell me everything about. He told me a lot, but he kept some things to himself.

That is where the self-compromising out of fear that he would leave me, began. If he liked some girl that got her nails done, I got mine done, or if he said so and so was more like this, I would try to be that. Somewhere I started to feel like I was not good enough for him, because he sought these external things. I wanted him to love and hold me up on a pedestal as much as I did him. I never understood how someone that loved him as much as I did could not be enough for him. He was focused - school was first, no girl would stop him from achieving that goal – not that I ever tried, but it somehow felt like if he loved me or showed me how much he did, or if he gave up the external things, I would somehow lead to his failure. That is why when I graduated, I moved to LA, to give our relationship time and space. This was one of the hardest choices that I made and one that I sometimes wish had been made differently.

When he graduated a year later we had a catastrophic break up over that dark skinned pretty girl with the hair – he wanted her at his graduation dinner – and me too. Before leaving from Los Angeles to go to DC, I asked him what his family was planning. His aunt and uncle owned a swanky Jamaican restaurant in Georgetown/ When he told me about the dinner, I specifically asked if his "friend" had been invited and he told me "no." I asked him to be honest because if she was, I wasn't getting on the plane… well she was invited and he told me at the graduation when there was nothing I could do – he took away my choice. When the graduates were seated, before the ceremony had started, I walked around looking for him, saying hi to my friends that I knew were graduating and when I found him, guess who he was sitting next to. The surprise on his face, the smirk on hers. We had a public break-up in front of people that I knew and loved – this time it was him breaking up with me, he was so cold, Friday she is coming to the dinner, my family knows her and invited her, if you do not like it then we are through – "F" it then. For the second time, I was on that campus crying, but this time I was broken – he had chosen someone else over me. I could not believe I had come across the country – with such excitement to see him, it had been months, and I was still so very much in love with him… for such a horrible let down.

I returned to Los Angeles, 3000 miles away from home, no family and very fragile. Ironic is as much as I was afraid of him leaving me, I left him to go to LA – years later he told me he did not understand how I could just leave. So much for things being said in real time, sometimes I wonder how things may have been different if he had told me some 20 years ago, but life is not always convenient. I wanted to love like that again. In terms of feelings and how I could feel for a man, he had set the bar; but at the same time, if I am honest, I did not really want to love like that again because I did not want to ever be hurt so deeply again. This is probably the first time I am being honest about that.

Whew. I think I will have a mint tea. Hot black tea, over crushed mint leaves, with orange honey to flavor, poured over some ice. Bitter sweet.

Unapologetically,

Friday

PART 4

THE PORN STAR

Posted on July 25, 2012

Exactly how does one react emotionally to a porn star with mama issues? I for the record, have no idea. I had the potential to love this dude, but he should have come with a sign that said 'let the buyer beware'. You know that kind of merchandise. You are in the store, looking at a great pair of jeans; the price tag reads slightly irregular and you stand there looking at it, trying to figure out what is wrong with it. That is how my relationship with the porn star was.

I met him at my friend's fiancé's album release party. My favorite track from these Washington High-school Graduates is "I Don't Give a Damn." It was a fun night in West Hollywood and I had on the hottest pair of white pants that I own. My hair was short and blonde at that time and he had well-manicured locks. He was quirky and funny, and yes, he had an amazing body. He was a writer's publishing rep and I was an account manager at a respected business management firm. We talked a little shop, he bought me a glass of wine, we chatted for a bit, exchanged business cards and went our separate ways; although I do remember him walking me to my car. To my surprise, he called me at the office the next day; and after a somewhat awkward conversation, he said something along the lines of I would like to get to know you and I do not mean professionally. I thought hmmm – let's call my music friends and get the skinny – everyone had nothing but nice things to say about him: He is so handsome, he is one of the nicest guys in the music game, you guys would make a really good couple, you both are such good people. So, I decided to let him take me on a date.

On the surface, he was smart, good looking, on his professional game, people that knew us both really pushed for our being a couple and it seems we had potential – financially, he was a mess and I think it bothered him that I had more material things than he did. Yet I drove a Ford and he drove a BMW – image was very important to him. He never really let me in, and I spent a lot of mental energy trying to figure things out. One minute he was taking me to his office's holiday party and introducing me to all kinds of music hot shots as his girl, and the next minute he needed space. He was living with a so-called ex-girlfriend and waiting for his lease to end so he could move out. When the lease ended – he stayed there at least another three months. He moved from a beautiful apartment in the Valley to a ROOM in his brother's fiancé's parent's guest house in Santa Monica. His reality was so far away from his name brand clothes, his name brand car, and his high-powered job that he did not know what to do.

Sex with him was amazing. He was a Cancer so he was sensitive and engaged during sex, he was something like a five-degree black-belt master, he was physically fit and limber as a gymnast. I remember one time where we were together and he asked me to do something, let's just call it Kamasutra Position #52. I was in awe of the mental control required to maintain that position, and I am a curvy girl, not some skin and bone chick. I later learned that all that control was his mask. The constant need to decompress, to practice his martial arts, he had more isms and fears than I care to express. He was a serial monogamist that only had the capacity to commit to his mother.

Like I said, I was constantly trying to figure him out and at some point, I stopped because I realized that it was not me. I had been a good girlfriend and it was him. He broke up with me the first time around; and again, I was left with this not understanding how I could be who I was and how I was and somehow not be good enough for this man. I did not realize how good his game was until our second time around. The way we broke up the first time was so random, the second time around I asked a LOT of questions. I wanted him to state what he wanted from a relationship with me so that I was clear. I asked if he was seeing anyone, and that is when he gave one of those subtle truths given by men that lie so much they forget – the beauty of time. He told me he was seeing someone from his past, but he only wanted to see me exclusively so that he would not be in the same position that he was before when he was seeing me and someone else – wtf? This Negro had admitted all be it two years after the fact that he was seeing me and his then ex-girlfriend. Again, me and a triangle. Well, when Christmas came around and he told me that he didn't want to invite me to his family's holiday dinner because he thought we were taking things slow, despite the fact that he knew my friends, my family, and my kids – hell no!

I called the fuckery for what it was and moved on all within three months. But before I did I sent a long email to his siblings, telling them their brother was a punk, that he has learned how to say the right things to women and has mastered being the nice guy, using their family as a perpetual carrot stick dangling – the greatest people on earth that you will never get to meet. This is why he is so controlled, because being the nice guy all the time, when you are a liar and manipulator takes an awesome amount of energy. As far as I am concerned, I am better than you and your whole entire family – I burned the bridge and we will never be friends again. If you were a true friend and not a punk ass, you would not run the bullshit game – you would be the motherfucker that could say I want my cake and you too…. And get it.

The Hollywood game does not work when your flash is generated from a room or upgraded to an apartment. I am not the chick that will keep fucking you because of the company you keep professionally.

I feel a Starbucks hot caramel macchiato calling me now with a heaping of sweet whipped crème on top…

Unapologetically,

Friday

PART 5

THE ACTOR

Posted on July 26, 2012

This last entry is a little delicate. My assignment was to think about how I have related emotionally in past relationships. Well this relationship is still current. And calls for a glass of red wine, maybe a Pinot Noir 2007 from the Russian River Valley in California.

The Actor – The way we met was a little surreal. Sundance Film Festival 2012, HBO Party at the Blue Iguana. Biz Markie was spinning. Black Hollywood was in the room, DeVon Franklin, Meagan Good, Michael K. Williams, Brickson Diamond, Jesse Williams, Michael Finely, Lorraine Tossaint, and Emayatzy Corinealdi. People were dancing and having a good time. I actually met an artist, Josiee Nadeau, whose work was displayed upstairs and she asked me to have a look at her work. I went upstairs to take a look –she had done beautiful original paintings of horses. At some point I was looking over the railing and I noticed this grey suit walking up the stairs – I had only seen him from behind and I thought *nice suit.* When he reached the top of the stairs, he turned into the crowd and walked around, when he reached the corner of the railing and turned the bend, I saw him from the front and I thought what a handsome presentation of a man. Tall, dark-skinned, very handsome – the black James Bond. Our eyes met and it was one of those moments where time stands still. From the distance, he gave the respectable head nod and I kindly nodded. This man made a B-line to me and the attorneys I was speaking with. He introduced himself to one of the women in the group that seemed to know him. He looked at me, flashed his Colgate smile with dimples, shook my hand and in his baritone voice introduced himself to me.

Him – *Are you an actress honey, because your look is screaming creativity?* Me – *No I get that a lot at festivals, I am an accountant.* Him – *Did you ever act?* Me – *no I did write two screenplays, but I found that writing took too much out of me emotionally so I put the pen down about ten years ago.* He asked me what my screenplays were about, we talked about where we were from – he lives one train stop from where I grew up in Brooklyn. He had a business degree that he felt helped him to better manage his career. It seemed like we just clicked – conversation was so easy. He was at Slamdance to promote the film he was in. He wrote his number down on one of the film's postcards. Him – *I want to keep in touch with you, and I don't mean for business.* Me – *I know. He walked me down stairs, helped check my coat out of the coat check and walked me to a cab.*

The next day on Main Street I stopped into a coffee book shop and I found a cute book called "Missed Connections" based on the

Craigslist classified ad where people that may have met someone at the grocery store and had an exchange, but did not act on the impulse to ask for a date – but they hope to find the person through a posting. This book had a collection of missed connections that were illustrated by Sophie Blackall. You see there was a catch to meeting him, because the universe has a sense of humor – he lives in NYC and I live in LA. I knew he would get the sentiment of the book. And when I saw him the next night for dinner before the Kickstarter party to celebrate his film – I gave him the book. I wrote a note "Do not let distance create a missed connection." He stared at me with those piercing eyes, and said I won't – thank you for this thoughtful gift Miss Lady. That was the beginning of finding love again.

I have learned that it is very important for me to keep my own identity when in a relationship. I have told him this. When my Great-grandmother passed away in February a lot was going on. I had a medical emergency that resulted in a huge loss of blood. My mom and best friend were finding me emergency care here in Los Angeles and trying to plan a funeral in Brooklyn. My brother was so concerned, he wanted to fly from Brooklyn to Los Angeles, unsure of if I should be doing anything other than resting. And I was determined to get to Brooklyn to bid farewell to my family's Matriarch. My kids thought I was dying. I thought I was dying, truth be told – but I told my kids I wasn't dying that day. Then I prayed "God please do not let me die." I phoned my new found friend to tell him I was on my way to the emergency room – and he told me what I needed to do to manage the situation until I could reach the hospital – he worked as an EMT overseas – duly noted. Thanks to vitamins, and two prescription drugs – I was able to get the bleeding under control, and I went to Brooklyn to bury my Great-grandmother. Guess who was with me, holding my hand.

I love this man – I am the most open and self-confident within this relationship than I have been since college. He likes the things about me that I can be self-conscious about, like the gap in my teeth, or my Buddha belly – but I like that he likes those physical parts of me. He is direct and confident with moments of being insecure, self-actualizing, and he is smart and a survivor of his own childhood challenges. I have such respect for him and for what he has accomplished with his life. He has great respect for women, thanks to growing up with three sisters, and I like that. I think if we had been in the same city, we would have been fast and furious and imploded by now – I told him that too. When I do not hear from him, or he falls off the radar, I feel anxious and I feel like he might leave or he might decide he does not love me anymore or he would prefer the company of some other woman over me (now that I type that – that is least probable because he is so cautious and particular). Funny is, sometimes, when he knows his work schedule has been crazy and we are distant, he will call me just to say I love you Friday. One day he even posted "Muuuaaahhh" on my Facebook page – I have never had a public remotely relationship anything posted on Facebook – ever by a man. As I sit here typing this – if I get anxious and start thinking – it is my self-esteem that comes to the front, and I will think, why is he not calling me, I feel so much for him, how can he not call me – truth is his not calling has nothing to do with me and has everything to do with where he is with work and with his family, and how much time and energy he has – none of which have anything to do with me or are things I can control. He actually knows all of my truths and loves me anyway.

When a man tells you go to the little girl in you to find your joys, and encourages you to pursue those loves – he is relating to you from another stratosphere. For me, he is talking to that inner child, the one with the bruises and scars… and she hears him.

Time for a super sweet bottle of Jamaican ginger beer, on ice, with a twist of mint leaves of course….so good. I am not big on soda, but a little fizz is good sometimes!

Unapologetically,

Friday

PART 6

LITTLE FRIDAY

Posted on July 27, 2012

I have recently come to the realization that I have not had very many relationships at least with the opposite sex, because I had children almost immediately after graduating college. Dating has not been something I really had an opportunity to do as a young single mom.

In concluding my first assignment, let's make a quick Sangria with some of the leftover Pinot Noir. Half glass wine, half glass cherry juice, 1/4 lime, 1/3 cup of frozen mixed berries, and 1 slice of an orange for color.

My walk away from this exercise is when I love people, I desperately want to know that they love me. I want them to tell me and show me so that I know, without a doubt, because I have an innate fear that if I love someone, they will not love me back – because I am somehow inadequate. I also loved very deeply and the man that I loved unconditionally had chosen someone other than me.

If I am my personal best – then I do not have to worry about being good enough. I watched the documentary "White Wash" yesterday and Andrea Kabwasa, at 30 learned to surf, and now she competes at a national level. She started surfing because she remembered how much fun it was as a kid so she decided to do it. The Actor told me to go back to the little girl inside of me and to remember the things that made me happy and go do whatever it is. I have been focusing on what makes Friday happy.

Now remember my assignment required me to journal – and Part 1-6 is what was journalized – in one night. My therapist received my very long journal and offered me her insights and I am sharing them with you. My purpose for doing this is to help someone who may also be on their road to self-discovery.

The Therapist:

My initial reaction is to say, the love that you so desperately are searching for is the love of SELF. Friday, deeply failing in love with Friday. The good, bad, and the ugly. When you do, your voice, style and expression will start to develop. The Actor, was absolutely right, start at the point where you as a child compromised to fit into the key influences of your life. Your mother, boyfriends, step father etc. Rewind, and then as an adult, tell your little self, it's okay. You (the adult you) will affirm her. You, the adult you, will love and validate her.

Unfortunately, our parents can only give us what they know to be true and honest, most of which is very limited. You're an adult, who has stumbled along the way to this time now. You've learned a lot on your own accord, without the love and validation from your mom or other key influences. Don't get me wrong, I know you love and care for your mom, but YOU, Ms. Friday have gone through the school of hard knocks and have picked yourself up ALL BY YOURSELF. The truth of the matter is we are ALL, in some way or another alone. We all desire to have someone to lean on and to share our lives with. But to get to a place of peace and joy, it's up to us, individually, to understand how to love ourselves, before we can expect another to totally understand how to love us and fill the gap of our needs. When we are anxious and worry about why someone else doesn't call us when we thought they should...when we expect them to fill the gap of warm fuzzies for us...we essentially are giving all power to them to control our emotionality. Fill yourself up with all the things that intrigue you, bring joy to you, and that offer a sense of curiosity. Go back and allow your little girl to show you the way. After all, she is' authentically you.

Now you all have an idea of why I am working with this therapist. I think her ability to hone in and speak to me in a language that I can understand is amazing. One night before going to bed I lay in my bed and my eyes started to get heavy and I day/night dreamed that I was a little girl in a white dress and The Actor was a little boy in a big white t-shirt, and we were walking on a wooded path. He was carrying a stick, and we reached a river bank to a slow moving river and he pulled down a huge green leaf and we climbed into it and drifted down the river as the sun shone on us. We were going home.

Little girl Friday is showing me the way. One of the things that I am doing is writing again. This blog for me is a breakthrough – I am averaging 1000 words per day, and unlike ten years ago, I am not crying and emotional, and feeling 20 emotions at one time, like a drug crazed mad woman. I am free, and I am pleased with me.

Unapologetically,

Friday

THE ISSUES

The mist was cold and dense and she could not see through the fog.

The Real Friday Jones

PART 1

ARTICULATE WHAT YOU MOST LOVE ABOUT YOU

Posted on July 28, 2012

"Life in The Color Blue"

I was born with a broken heart... until now I knew not why. But a grown man kissed the lips hidden between a six year old's hips just yesterday. Then the same man would hold a knife and threatened to take her mother's life as if beating her black and blue was not enough of a sacrifice, but she was six so what could she do? And then German Measles attacked in high-school in that first trimester that only she knew contained a life devastated while it was so new and so she had to choose... like so many women do. And she cared for him enough to birth two of his babies just to hear him say you are not good enough for me... bitch. Her father died, never present, not knowing. And those were just stories from her life....

Then she turned on the news and a 24-year-old Nigerian woman was to be stoned to death under Sharia Law for conceiving a child out of wedlock. She opened the Wall Street Journal and read how an 11-year-old girl from Niger was pulled out of school by her father who in his mind could not support her anymore, so he married her off to a 24-year-old boy who would only abandon her after she delivered a stillborn child born of his seed.

Then PBS airs a show on "The Children of the Brothels" babes born to circumstance that is not of their doing, to women who based on caste, income, or a lack thereof, are left with no choice but to exist...

And Rwanda, Darfur, Blood Diamonds, Video Vixens, Child Brides... she cries. India Arie " I am ready for love, why are you hiding from me" A better question why are you hiding from the whole world to see.....

She was called a wounded healer, and her soul still bleeds, waiting for the rebirth of femininity. She was born with a broken heart...and now she knows why.

- **Friday**

This is a poem I wrote years ago. I felt it represented who I am. For people, wanting to know me, this is like a litmus test. Can you handle all of this, because this is the real me? Are your eyes sensitive enough to see to my soul? Or is my hard exterior the depth of your vision? In the spiritual world a congenital heart condition means in this life that person will have self-love issues to be resolved during this lifetime. "Congenital" by definition means having a particular trait from birth. Interestingly the teenage uncle that attempted to rape me had the same heart condition as me, except his surgical scar keyloided and looked like a tree on his chest – out of all of my grandfather's sons, he felt he was the least loved. I remember as a kid he always seemed to be defending himself. My son also has the same heart condition, and I have wrapped him up with my words so he knows he is loved.

My next assignment from the therapist was to "articulate what most do you love about YOU." YIKES!!!! I am the person that takes care of everyone else. I take care of my two children, I take care of my clients' needs and issues, I am co-director of a youth cheerleading team, the SYFL Crenshaw Colts and I take care of paperwork, budgeting, scheduling. I do not even have a proper bathtub when I want Calgon to take me away, and now the therapist wants me to focus on myself. Needless to say I did not jump all over this assignment. I contemplated it for about two weeks before I actually put pen to paper. My response to the assignment resulted in the following email to the therapist:

I have been a struggling a bit with this last exercise for several reasons.

- I composed a list of things that I like about myself and when I looked at it, it seemed like it was short – like there should be more. So I asked my daughter who is 14 to do the same thing (which she has not) but I wanted to see by contrast how would a girl whose childhood was very different from mine, and whose confidence I made sure to build up – how her list would be different. Well I do not have an answer, because she did not do what I asked. When I look at myself in the mirror – I am at times amazed at how pretty I am. When I wake up in the morning I wake up, with no makeup and I look amazing – but I do not always feel like the woman I see in terms of confidence. Sometimes when I am dressed the way I want to be, I walk out the front door looking and feeling like a million bucks. But then as every day is a constant struggle, I feel weak and can drop a tear instantly. So I do like the way I look, I have a really nice smile and nice eyes. I can be witty and fun and sometimes even funny. I like that I am book smart. I like how I feel when I listen to good music. I like how well I communicate with others. I like connecting with nature, hiking or water sports. I like that I know how to swim. I love cooking meals for friends and family. And I like to be social more than being a recluse. I like that I have many ideas – I wish I knew how to monetize. And although I do a lot of complaining about my kids – I actually love being around children.

- The other part of this assignment that has been a challenge is going back to the "little girl" in me and allowing her to be a "guide" if you will. There are so many things that I would like to do, and everything boils down to money. There was a time when my best friend and I stopped doing some things together, because I could not afford it. We both wanted to take a photography class – I really like taking pictures and I wanted to learn how to take better pictures – but I could not afford the required camera for the class. We both wanted to take pole dancing, but at $800 a month, this single mom did not have that kind of disposable income. I would love to take dance and painting classes – and my current financial situation is actually more than I can bear at times. As much as I would love to explore different things, I am at a place where I cannot and there is not much joy in my life right now. I carry sadness like it's a friend. And trying to keep a good spirit and be positive changes by the moment. One moment I am being positive, the next I am crying myself to sleep. The life energy that I am putting out right now, with clients, the business, my kids, trying to find a job – everything is survival – there is not much right now that returns to me in the form of stability, financial well-being, or time to explore things for me and my growth. There is a lot going out, but not enough coming back in that brings balance right now. So what would make Friday whole/ happy/ fall in love with herself? I do not have the time or money to find out. Last night, all I could do for myself was burn a candle and an incense and try to be happy about it. If I could unshed the bulk of my responsibilities, I would say," You folks take these kids." I would go maybe get some job in retail – mindless work, and take time to figure me out for a while – but for some reason when you say that to people,

> they go "things will get better.... God does not give you more than you can bear". And I always think, *can I tell you that I can't bear it anymore?* And it would be sufficient, instead of waiting for a postmarked letter from God.... I am just saying...

I don't know where we go from here or what my next assignment is, but I am still going to try self-discovery, despite my many challenges. It is time to grow. Truth is, growing hurts. I remember what growing pains felt like as a kid, and the aches in my legs would keep me up half the night, crying – not much has changed.

Now that some time has passed, I realize a couple of things – I used the word love twice in that entry, which is a little sad. The idea that money can prohibit one from personal growth is silly – I might not be able to take two classes per week at $15/ per class right now the way that I want to – to unleash my inner dancer; but if I speak to my inner-child, here is a truth from my own reality. When I was a child, I really wanted to be a choreographer and an actress. I thought I would be a great choreographer because of the way I felt and visualized music – it did not matter to me that much that I was not the best dancer. In the 5th grade there was a city wide dance audition for an after school program that was going to be taught by a woman names Sister Cole. I went to the audition with a couple of friends and I was horrible. I did not make the cut. But one of my friends did. I went with her to the first day of class with Sister Cole, now Sister Cole was like the

Debbie Allen character from Fame. She was tough as nails and you had to earn her respect. She was going down the attendance list, she asked if there was anyone on the list whose name she did not call as she stood towering over me with her huge afro, looking me dead in my eyes. I raised my hand, she asked "who are you?" I told her my name and said I did not make the cut but I want to dance. She looked at me and said "if you miss one class, I will cut you from this list." I never missed a class.

Right now money is tight – tighter than I care for it to be. But if Little Friday has taught me anything it is that money is not the only means; and if you look for a way, you may just find a way. So for now – I plug my computer up to the flat-screen television in my living room whenever I feel like it, and I take all kinds of dance classes. I still do not think I am particularly good, but who cares, I am living my dream. That was not the last class I talked myself into as a kid; now I am talking to me, and I am listening. My blender is loud as I toss in a handful of ice, 4oz whole milk and a healthy scoop of strawberry ice cream... reminds me of the good times.

Unapologetically

Friday

PART 2

THE FEAR OF TELLING

Posted on July 29, 2012

Last night I attended an International Friend Festival, hosted by two of my dearest friends. My friend's husband bartended specialty drinks and there is one that I tried called The All American which was worth sharing. 1/2 Coconut Vodka, 1/4 Grenadine, 1/4 Blue Curacao, over ice. Perfect summer treat.

I was not sure how The Therapist was going to react to my issues with the last assignment. This is part one of her two-part response, which I received via email:

The Therapist

Ms. Friday, you need to be a writer. You definitely have a story to tell. In fact, I would think about writing with the intention of putting it in a "play" format. There is a HUGE story to tell here that is relatable. The stories that most families don't want to talk about...sex, incest, the expression of pain. The command to stuff the emotions, the fear of "telling". This behavior has infiltrated many, many families. The story also shows the journey, your journey to understanding yourself. I think because of your writing skills, a book or play collaboration may be your ticket to real self-independence. Ms. Friday, you have a lot to share and say as you overcome. I think journaling, or blogging is very therapeutic. It is a therapeutic tool. Is it an open blog??? I personally would not blog as an open forum. For your experience and ideas can be and should be used for your own good. That is to put and use in a collaborative way. I so appreciate you sharing these notes with me. It so confirms, what I have sensed all along.

I was pleased that the therapist re-affirmed that I should be a writer. It is what I came to Los Angeles for, it is why I lived across the street from Sony Studios, so I could be reminded of my creativity. Last week I watched the first episode of "The Hypnotist" written by actor J. August Richards. It is an amazing intro to a web-series that I hope will wind up on television. Due to confidentiality I cannot speak much about the details, but there is a writer who feels confined like he has no voice – this is how much of my life has felt on some level.

How does pain express in a child sexualized too young, how is pain expressed when a child sees their mother beaten by a mad man, how does pain express after an attempted rape by a family member, how does pain express when you move from a place of safety to places of uncertainty, how does pain express when your trust of men is diminished and then you are introduced to your father at age 10, how does pain express when being smart is a curse of sorts, how is pain expressed when you are unaware that you are a beautiful human being?

Before my mother married my step-father, I knew I did not like him. I did not know why. She had other boyfriends that I did like, but there was something about this guy that did not sit well with me. At that time, I lived on Saratoga Avenue and Chauncey Street and I had a friend that lived on Chauncey – we were in the second grade, I believe. I told her that I did not like him and I was running away. She said, well you cannot go by yourself, I will go with you. The next day I wore two dresses to school so I could have a change of clothes and a coat. I remember that I took my favorite dress which had an orange top, with a white rounded peter pan collar, gold buttons, and a grey pleated skirt. My friend and I left school together, I did not have much of a plan, we played after school in the school yard like normal, and then instead of walking home, we walked until dusk. Just when darkness seemed real, a woman walking down the street said, aren't you so and so's daughter. I told her yes. She asked me what was I doing so far from home, I said I did not know. She told me and my friend to about-face because my home was the other way. By the time I got home, my mother was in tears and frantic. She asked me where I was and I told her I was running away. I did not think she loved me any more since "he" came. She hugged me. Surprisingly, I did not get a whooping, and she told me she loved me, I was important, I did not need to feel that way, no one would ever take my place. That may have been the last bit of normal.

And just to give you a clear understanding of my reality, I had a Jewish teacher that hated me. We lived in what might be considered a predominantly black, working-class neighborhood. The school wanted to skip me, but my brother was in the 3rd grade, and my mom did not want me in his class, my birthday also falls early, so it already seemed like I was younger than most of my classmates. Unfortunately for me, it took this second grade teacher strangling me during a school play rehearsal for me to be moved out of her class. My mother was adamant about not telling her business or the business of what went on in the house. I had a somewhat impossible situation. I learned early to not tell, to not speak up for myself, to self- sacrifice, to protect people that were not worthy of my protection, to be responsible for shit that was not my responsibility – all at the age of six.

As a result of being sexualized too young, I was body conscious. I started having sex in the 8th grade, I remember not enjoying it, feeling cold, and that was before I knew anything about condoms, so the pull out method often resulted in me laying in cold semen. I tried to talk to my mother before actually having sex and all she could offer was if you get pregnant, I will put you out. That was not effective, because it did not address what I was feeling for this boy that probably had feces tracks in his draws. The first time someone tried to give me head, it felt gross, it reminded me of being a little girl and I did not like it. By the time I got into high school I was dating college boys and the pressure to have sex was more than I could bear, I did not know how to say no. Sometimes with my high school boyfriend, I would lay there, not participating, in silent protest; and I would be upset with myself if I climaxed – even when not participating. Sex was distorted and I had no power in my sexuality, until college.

I was, and probably still am guarded. On that night where I thought my stepfather would kill us all, I swore, I would never let a man put his hands on me. If he did, I promised myself that I would kill him. I came dangerously close to keeping that promise. The father of my children is seven years my senior, and he was a rebound from the college boyfriend. He is not someone I would have chosen, but I was 3000 miles from home and lonely – he was available. Sex lead to pregnancy, I was asked to abort, and if you read my poem, I had already been there and done that – abortion is not birth control and I was not going through that again. In an effort to keep this short, I moved home pregnant, returned to LA with my son, with hopes of becoming a writer, only to have my plans thwarted by my kids' father's, ultra-Christian parents that wanted us to get married and live as a family. Their plan resulted in my daughter's birth. Neither of us really wanted to be together, and one day under the pressure of it all, he lost his mind and during an argument, he at 6'0" strangled my 5'3" self over a couch with my son and his son watching and crying in horror. I scratched his face as if I were a cat and I started plotting my exit. I did not want to go to jail for killing someone I did not even want to be with and jeopardize my ability to parent my children. I knew I would kill him, and when his ultra-Christian mother called me, not to ask if I was okay, but to inquire why I had scratched her son's face the way I did, I told her scratches were preferable to his being dead. Shortly after, I moved out with no regrets.

When my family returned to New York after our two-year stint in Virginia, I thought things would be better. I thought I would reconnect with my old friends, but we lived with my grandmother in Bed-Stuy, and the school around the corner from her house was my new school. The girls at this school were huge, there was one super mean girl that had two fingers on her left hand. She and her crew of mean girls chased me home every day, until I finally stood up for myself. They did not like my southern twang and they did not like that our teacher had taken a liking to me because I was smart and did my homework timely. It seemed like turn after turn as a child, there was no peace.

Then there was the slow introduction of my father. My father is Muslim, as is half of my family. I was so jaded by men at that time, that I hated him for not being present, for not knowing everything that had happened to me. My mother kept us away from him because, when we were infants, he threatened to kidnap us and take us to Pakistan to be raised Muslim. It was not until she felt that we were old enough that she allowed him to see us. I was a thorn in his side at every meeting. I was not mature enough to tell him my life's story, and I was also angry with him for not being there. I thought if he had been clued into his children, despite his ex-wife moving on to a new husband, he would have known that the new husband was in my panties at night time. I was so angry and unforgiving with him. It also did not help that as a Muslim, my father had a new wife every couple of years. By the time I got to college, I told him I was not interested in meeting any more of his wives, and I was not interested in getting to know him, because it seemed to me that all he did was run through women, good women. My Father died February 2006, I believe. I went to him on his death bed. He had suffered his second stroke, and in order to make some sort of peace with him, even though he was already practically gone from his body – I told him my life's story. I told him he owed it to me and my children to protect us when he passed on.

I remember walking by the J Train, near the Gates Avenue stop and I ran into this boy that I knew from before moving to Virginia. I think I was in high-school at the time. He looked at me and asked if it was really me, I said yes. He was like, I remember you – I remembered him too, all of the girls thought he was cute, even then. He said, if I knew you would grow up to look like this, I would have been nicer to you – his words did not sound like the Music Soul Child song. His words made me think *your loss idiot,* and I was turned off. He asked if we could keep in touch and wrote his number down. I threw it away before I got home. To this day, I do not like men to come on to me solely based on how I look, or how sexy they think I am. Those type of men think my sex is somehow theirs to conquer and it is not. My beauty radiates on both the inside and the outside and it is not tied to my sex. Men, just because you think I am pretty is not reason enough for me to want to fuck you or make love to you. There is so much more to me than the sexy you think you see.

Unapologetically,

Friday

PART 3

THE THERAPIST DISSECTS ME

Posted on July 30, 2012

This entry is the second part of The Therapist identifying the issues. For now, I will let her analysis stand on its own. When I read it initially I was at my office at 1:30AM working and wrapping my desk. I remember looking out the window and there were no cars driving down the street when I read her response. I was alone, and as her words spoke to me, I cried, and I released.

The Therapist

Your struggles are related to your self-concept. Understanding the core of who you are. It was never defined as a child from the primary caregivers. You didn't receive the basics that would help you to identify your purpose, that you were loved, and that you were worthy to be protected. No one came to rescue you. No one comforted you. No one validated you. You were a victim of a horrible situation. Not only in the home, but also in the school. Who could you as a child turn to for protection, guidance, support. You were a violated child who lived in a hostile environment.

You've been running from hostile environments, ever since. Poor relationships, poor job experiences, especially this last job where you didn't feel appreciated. Entering in relationships, and demanding pretty quickly for them to state their intentions. It's like a flashback of the conversations you had with your step father, never really understanding what their intentions were, but knowing it was a frightening experience and you needed to somehow, mostly mentally protect yourself. That is where your strong defenses came from.

The forgiveness first comes with you forgiving little Friday. By telling her in a letter how proud you, the adult Friday is for little Friday staying strong and surviving. She survived Friday, and she survived with amazing skill. Little Friday came through this experience helping the adult Friday to develop a heart to serve and help others.

The adult Friday has to finish the journey of cleansing. The blogging will be good for that. And once it has been completely released, the new story needs to be re-defined. It will take a while for the release and the redefining to reconcile, but it will. Allow for each new day to bring new clarity.

Know, that the external world will never give you what you want and deserve and that is validation. But yet, you have measured the value of your validation, your worth, in terms of how successful you are financially. You're a success Friday. The fact that you are still here, healthy and whole. The fact that you have raised two kids, independently. The fact that you are in business...and knew how to put it all together, renders in my eyes that you are a success.

But somewhere in your mind's eye, you are saying, perhaps subliminally, that "you are not good enough". Behind that million-dollar confident look, and beautiful smile, is a soul and spirit that is unsettled. The flesh has ruled with the things that you thought would bring happiness, degrees, credentials, freedom; but as you stated, it is only a short lived emotion/feeling, bringing tears of sadness. You've embraced the sadness of your younger years where you did not have control. Instead you must learn how to embrace life from the endless possibilities.

Friday, needs to spend time with Friday understanding who you are. What are your core values? What makes you tick? How can you have a long list of positive things about you when you project out, not from within?

When you finally forgive and release your primary experiences you will then learn to grow and love yourself better. Then you'll be able to stop defining your successes from a financial point of view. Then you'll learn to appreciate self-validation.

When you move away from the victim status, which I believe you're starting to do now, you will see that you will re-define yourself differently. Once you re-define yourself differently and move away from the negative schemes, more positive events will come to you. But it is your soul and spirit that need to be developed and take center stage.

Individuals who still believe that their past defines their future will never have a future full of possibilities. Individuals who don't believe their past defines their future will have a future full of creative opportunities by re-narrating and re-defining where they see themselves going. Your experiences still hurt, for your voice until now was never expressed regarding it. And the most painful thing is the person who didn't protect you; your mom, is the very person who you still hold on to, and or at this point may even depend on. There's a painful conflict there, for the expression of your true and authentic self, is still being limited.

Again, you are able to externalize/ project the external things about yourself, and, with that, you're well pleased. I'm pretty, I'm smart, I'm a giver, I'm social, I like to cook for friends; but beneath that, Ms. Friday is a person who has not reconciled your experiences of your primary years. Those feelings still subliminally haunt you. Why else would you get up at 4:30 am in the morning and journal on your blog? You're still holding on to those years, because not until now, have you developed the strength to articulate your experience. The journaling and the blogging are a well-needed catharsis. You need to continue to do so, until your full story has been told.

I am going to order the material that I want you to work through. This will give you a better concept of what you're experiencing. No charge Ms. Friday, just pay me back when you become famous, which I know you will.

WOW. It will take me at least seven entries to delve into everything that The Therapist has said here. But I want these words to marinate for you like a glass of strawberry lemonade: 4-5 large strawberries, half a lemon, sweeten with sugar to taste, 6 oz water, and ice – blend together in a blender. I prefer to let it sit for at least 5 hours – it seems to taste better once the flavors have gelled together.

Savor the flavors.

Unapologetically,

Friday

PART 4

UNDERSTANDING YOUR SELF CONCEPT

Posted on August 1, 2012

"Your struggles are related to your self-concept. Understanding the core of who you are. It was never defined as a child from the primary care givers. You didn't receive the basics that would help you to identify your purpose, that you were loved, and that you were worthy to be protected. No one came to rescue you. No one comforted you. No one validated you. You were a victim of a horrible situation. Not only in the home, but also in the school. Who could you as a child turn to for protection, guidance, support? You were a violated child who lived in a hostile environment."

I almost do not even know where to begin with this – "Your Struggles are related to your self-concept." What the heck is a "self-concept?" You know, I remember a time when life was good – I remember music on Saturday mornings and cleaning the house, I remember Shirley Chisholm Pre-school and male teachers in dashikis and afros, I remember drums at pre-school, and singing "Lift Every Voice and Sing," I remember learning the principles of Kwanzaa, I remember a time I could do no wrong because we lived in the neighborhood that my mother grew up in – and everyone knew who I was. If I stepped out of line, my mother knew before she got home. I remember my mom taking us on dates to Coney Island and riding in a Cadillac where I was able to sit in her lap, or her boyfriend's lap, and drive. I remember all of the good food. I remember life being good. And then it changed.

When it changed, my memory is sketchy at best. I lived in Virginia for two years. Outside of the kids that lived on our block and the bus driver we had for school, I do not remember any teachers, friends, school activities. It is as if that time did not exist. The only day I kind of remember about school was sitting in the back of the classroom and spacing out, and I remember the teacher calling my mother to tell her that she thought I should be tested because I seemed retarded. I remember my mother saying something to the effect of, 'Friday has always been gifted, maybe she is bored.' I do not know if I was bored, but I was gone. The only color I remember from those two years was playing with the kids on the block, racing pine straws down the gutter, catching bees, swimming at the public pool in the summer, picking fruit from trees in the neighborhood and riding our bikes to the lake. I draw a complete blank when it comes to school. I remember the bus driver because she did not take any horseplay on her bus. She challenged us to think about our behavior and who we wanted to be in life. I also remember my mom giving the best of what she had to give, she always made a big deal out of birthdays and holidays. Our worst Christmas was the one I remember the most, she told us that we were not going to have a Christmas like we were accustomed to, there were not going to be many toys because we could not afford it. I really did not expect anything that Christmas, but she got us a Rubix Cube and a coloring book. My brother and I were so happy that we had something. During this time my home life was safe, I remember things surrounding home – school must have been hostile – I have no recollection of what the school was like – NONE. I do not know what I may have wanted to be – but I know I wanted to go back home to what I knew to be normal, to where I felt safe.

According to Wikipedia "**Self-concept** (also called **self-construction, self-identity** or **self-perspective**) is a multi-dimensional construct that refers to an individual's perception of "self" in relation to any number of characteristics, such as academics (and non-academics), gender roles and sexuality, racial identity, and many others. Each of these characteristics is a research domain (i.e. Academic Self-Concept) within the larger spectrum of self-concept although no characteristics exist in isolation as one's self-concept is a collection of beliefs about oneself. While closely related with self-concept clarity (which "refers to the extent to which self-knowledge is clearly and confidently defined, internally consistent, and temporally stable"), it presupposes but is distinguishable from self-awareness, which is simply an individual's awareness of their self. It is also more general than self-esteem, which is a function of the purely evaluative element of the self-concept."

By the fourth grade, I do not think I had a self-concept, I think I was only self-aware. I did not like being a girl. Being a girl meant that you were prey for the predatory behavior of men and boys. Men got to fish, which I thought was fun, women had to scale, gut, and cook the fish, which was not fun. I remember it was important to my mother that we look a certain way, she as a parent was not to look better than her kids. We were always well-groomed. My mother hated musicals, so my interest in singing and dancing were not really acknowledged, although she did place me in the band as a baton twirler, and she placed me in track for first and second grade. As I am typing this entry, I feel a little bad. It seems like knowing who my mother is, like she would have affirmed certain things, but I honestly do not remember. If she did, perhaps I did not believe her.

As an adult I really struggle with the concept of faith, and believing that things will somehow be okay, just on sheer faith. When I feel a lack of control, particularly over outcomes where I seem to be doing the best that I know how to do, when I do not feel safe in my circumstance – anxiety is an unwanted companion. I do know how fucked up things can be. I know what struggle is. I know how to count on me and when I cannot save the day, I do not know how to ask for help or how to confide in friends – I did not know how to ask for help as a child. I protected my mom in ways that no child should be asked, and there was no-one to rescue me. My mom did not know, she did not know I needed to be comforted and validated. The idea of being worthy of being protected, implies that someone was protecting me – and my mother did, based on what she knew. But she did not know that I was more fragile than I showed on the outside. I needed so much more than I received – and nobody knew, not my mother, and not my father.

When we returned to Brooklyn, in the 5th and 6th grades, we lived with my grandmother. In the 7th grade we lived with my mom's best friend's boyfriend, but we had our own space. In the 8th grade we moved to where Bed-Stuy meets Bushwick. I remember my mother asked her brother – the one she grew up with to baby-sit me. I remember telling her I did not want to be left alone with him. This uncle is the sweetest of all hearts and has never harmed a hair on my head. She asked me if he had ever done anything to me or ever touched me, and I told her truthfully, no, he had not. She asked me why didn't I want to be left alone with him – and the truth was when I had been left alone with men, I had been violated, and I did not want to be put in that situation again, where I would have to defend myself – even if she felt that in this case, her brother could be trusted. Her trust had been broken before, and I had been the one to pay the price. How is a 12- year-old child supposed to articulate that? So my response was I don't know why, but I do not want to be left alone with him, I would rather be left home alone.

So again, self-concept – what is a self-concept? I am now defining my self-concept. I am defining who I am. I do love myself. I want to fall in love with me. There is only one of me, and I am worthy of validation, protection and comfort from me. For a time, I really wanted someone to save me; I wanted a husband that would take my burdens away. Despite the fact that I have depended on me for a mighty long time, the harsh truth is that as an adult I am responsible for me, I am responsible for my happiness, I am responsible to be who I want to be, and it is okay if not everyone likes that me – so long as I love that me.

Let's close out with a childhood favorite, good old fashioned chocolate milk. 8oz 2% Low-fat milk, mix in Nestle Quick chocolate powder to taste – enjoy!!!

Unapologetically,

Friday

PART 5

RUNNING FROM HOSTILE ENVIRONMENTS

Posted on August 2, 2012

"You've been running from hostile environments, ever since. Poor relationships, poor job experiences, especially this last job where you didn't feel appreciated. Entering in relationships, and demanding pretty quickly for them to state their intentions. It's like a flash back of the conversations you had with your stepfather, never really understanding what their intentions were, but knowing it was a frightening experience and you needed to somehow, mostly mentally protect yourself. That is where your strong defenses came from."

Running from hostile environments... The Therapist has hit the nail on the head. I have been running from hostile environments, looking for peace since I was about 7-years-old. Trying to get to a home environment that was reflective of how I see myself. The first job I had out of college gave me the opportunity to work for some of the most established names in music in the mid 90's. The reason I was hired was because I was black, and had an accounting degree in an all-white business management practice in the heart of Times Square. The managing partner, who is now Jay-Z's manager/ financial advisor, genuinely loved hip-hop and R&B music. It was important to him that he had a competent black person on his team because 95% of his client base were heavy hitters.

Unfortunately, his needs were not reflective in my pay. I started out making $25K in 1993. I was sent to California in 1994 to work in the tax department of this firm's corporate office for one year. I returned to New York, and did not receive even a cost of living increase. When I returned to New York I was pregnant with my son, and that firm's human resources department did not even ensure that my health care benefits were in place – knowing I was pregnant. The human resource department did not transfer my California medical coverage to New Jersey, so I was pregnant with no medical coverage. I had to do the legwork to get a group opened by Met Life in New Jersey where I lived. It was so stressful – down to the last vacation I had planned before my son was born at 29 weeks. My vacation time was approved and then the tax manager said I had to work, because something he forgot to place on his calendar was the same weekend and I needed to come in. WTF? My son was born that weekend – the weekend I had allowed for myself to rest. That was the camel's straw. When I went into early labor, knowing how my three years at this company manifested with no raise, added stress, clearly little respect – mentally I was done. Shortly after I returned to work after my maternity leave, I gave notice to work for a freelance producer, doing production management for music videos.

The freelance producer. This guy was a mess. He was the soon to be brother-in-law of one of my college friends. He was Jamaican. He and his brother wanted to get into filmmaking with the Persaud Brothers and Mekhi Pfiefer. I negotiated contracts, kept their production books clean – and then I became too trusting and believing in getting the job done. I rented a 15 passenger van on my credit card, the producer and his brother never reimbursed me, I had to take them to court. When I saw that the micro budget project was not going well, I pulled all of the original invoices in the production book, made copies for the investor/ producers and told them I did not think the film was in good hands. These wanna-be Jamaican mobsters actually threatened me – they were going to kill me. Really? My brother is known internationally and you and your Long Island crew are going to do what? This fool's brother had the nerve to ask if my son was family, because he could not understand why nothing was being done to me. How about I am highly favored!

I returned to work for a recycling company for about one year, and then I decided to follow my dream of wanting to be a TV Writer and I moved from New Jersey to Los Angeles. Unfortunately, I had let the grandparents of my son convince me to move in with them to save money. I gave up an apartment on the belief that these people would make their home available to me and my son, as I pursued finding a job. I flew my son to Los Angeles, then I flew back to New Jersey to pick up my car, packed it with all of my worldly possessions and drove across the country by myself. The day I arrived in Los Angeles, North Long Beach to be specific, this man's parents had decided with their god, that as Christians, families belonged together and I needed to take my child to their son's house so that we could be a family. WTF? Could you people in your brilliance had told me that before I came to Los Angeles? Who does that? I cannot believe that they essentially forced their religious views on me to the point where they took away life defining choices. Their son had not made any proposal of marriage to me, and honestly, I was never in love with him. Truth be told, his parents should be ashamed of themselves, because they knew that their son was not an honorable man; and it certainly was not my job to turn him into an honorable man.

Eventually, I found a job back in business management and I was there for 12.5 years. I was able to float between the tax department and bookkeeping. I worked on some of the highest net worth individuals of the firm. In two cases my performance was responsible for increasing retainers from $10K per month to $15K per month and in another instance from $12K to $17K. For one client I replaced his CFO, I found the client almost $140K in rental escalations, that the CFO had not collected in years. The CFO made $150K and at the time I possibly was making $55K-$60K. I learned my professional worth. Unfortunately, after taking the Senior Partner and the Junior Partner out for lunch to ask what is the plan for me after twelve years, I was basically told there was none. The Senior Partner even went so far as to tell me sometimes you have to leave a place and learn before you can have what you want. WTF?

Unfortunately for me, this was about the time that I had met a con-man, who could have a whole chapter to his Thom Foolery, and this man who had met the Senior Partner one week prior at a book signing, called the Senior Partner and threatened him on the day that I received a criminal report that clearly let me know he was a con. I faxed the criminal report from my office to a bank in North Carolina – I remembered meeting the banker and something did not feel right about the meeting. I told the banker, I thought he should know who he was doing business with. My gut was right on because the con-man had submitted my name on a loan application the day before. After the threat to the Senior Partner, I was asked to not come in for a week, the entire staff was on lock down for one day. The day The Con Man called my office, he also called and threatened me and my life. I was so afraid, I called the US Marshalls to see if I could be escorted home. This man was nuts, he had coned me and an investment group out of $65K I was terrified, and again no-one came to the rescue.

When I was told to leave the office, no one offered to simply walk me to my car. I only had me to depend on. The firm took the threats seriously; the staff was told to not talk to me or so much as look at me when I returned to work. I had been purposely isolated, my clients had been called and were asked if they had noticed any mishandling of their finances, and to report any discrepancies. My years of credibility were in question because I had been a victim to a vicious con. I had one of the worst reviews I had ever had in my entire 12 years. I was told that my performance was sub-par and that I should consider getting new clients. How do those two statements belong together? I played their game, sent out an announcement saying I had been given the opportunity to acquire my own clients, then I asked the Managing Partner, what did he want me to convey during these meetings about the firm. I also asked them for copies of my reviews for the past 12 years – they could only produce one written review that glowed. I knew and they knew they wanted to fire me, but they had no basis to fire me and they would have opened themselves up to a huge lawsuit. Then I started bringing my ass back to the conference room where people took lunch breaks – I ended the artificially imposed isolation. I re-read the "48 Laws of Power" by Robert Greene and started taking back my power. Then I started planning my exit.

Over the course of time I have told my closest of friends and family the stories of my life, and they say – only this stuff happens to you Friday. I had a woman tell me that in my past life as a nun, I had written my life's story but placed the story under a stair case, and I was sad that the story of my life had never been published. Well thanks to technology in this life, and all of these various experiences, I have had a rich life and I freely share it with you. The good, bad, and the ugly – it is published here for you. I refuse to run from any more hostile environments, and I refuse to attract any hostile environments or people to me. As I discover my truest voice, I rise unashamed of these experiences and I leave them in yesterday where they belong in the name of universal love, and I grow.

This is actually worthy of celebrating. Barefoot makes a wonderful Brut Cuvee' – let's pop the bottle and toast to new beginnings.

Unapologetically,

Friday

PART 6

RELEASE YOUR PRIMARY EXPERIENCES

Posted on August 3, 2012

"Know, that the external world will never give you what you want and deserve and that is validation. But yet, you have measured the value of your validation, your worth, in terms of how successful you are financially. You're a success, Friday. The fact that you are still here, healthy and whole. The fact that you have raised two kids, independently. The fact that you are in business…and knew how to put it all together, renders in my eyes that you are a success…When you finally forgive and release your primary experiences, you will then learn to grow and love yourself better. Then you'll be able to stop defining your successes from a financial point of view. Then you'll learn to appreciate self-validation."

The Therapist keeps casting pearls, are you swine or are you wisdom? When I say she has dissected me to a tee – I mean she has dissected me to a tee. Forgiving and releasing my primary experiences…. hmmm. Moving as frequently as we did, disturbed my peace growing up. It affected my sense of belonging, primarily because there was no apparent reason for all of the transition. It was years later, I was an adult, by the time my mother told me that part of our misfortune was because of one of her best friends that she had planned to move to Washington DC with, reneged on the move, leaving my mother out to dry financially. She had given up a stable Job at Merrill Lynch, she had given up our apartment in Brooklyn, she was leaving the crazy man she had married, she could not afford the apartment in DC by herself, so the two weeks in Virginia that was supposed to help facilitate this move, became the beginning of a terrible downward spiral from which my mother could not quickly recover – it had taken my primary years and the damage had unfortunately been done.

Two of the things that I most wanted as a child was our own house and to have money because I did not like feeling poor, I did not like knowing we were poor and struggling to survive, where a mayonnaise sandwich had to do as dinner sometimes. I had the deceitful life expectation that because I was smart, if I got a good job, I could find financial success. My life expectation should have been to make happiness my goal. To follow my heart's desires. But oftentimes with my life choices, it seemed as if I kept stubbing my toe, and every time there was healing, or growing with one step, then I would stub my toe again. As a young adult, especially without a mentor, there was serious lack of direction for my life.

Had I pursued happiness, I would have taken acting as a minor at Howard University. If I had not defined myself so much by merely experiencing love and a sense of safety from my College Boyfriend, I would have broken up with him before graduating from Howard and looked for a more stable reflection of love and happiness. Had I pursued happiness, I would have walked away from business management where the primary responsibility is to take care of other people, and bear responsibility for other people's problems and missteps, and I would have found a career that fed my soul joy on a daily basis. Fear steered many of my life choices and decisions made based on fear are wrong 100% of the time. And so, right now as I write this blog entry, I forgive myself for not knowing how to choose happiness. I forgive myself for trying to be the good girl to get a degree in four years in a major that she was good at but not in love with. I forgive myself for not knowing how to love myself enough to be courageous and to do better. The wells of my eyes are filled with tears, and I forgive myself. I leave any of my life's regrets on these pages because I sincerely did the best that I knew how to do with the emotional tools that I had. And like they say in church, if there is anyone out there that needs forgiveness, I forgive you and please love yourself enough in this moment to forgive yourself too.

For my 40th Birthday, I flew my mother, grandmother, and kids to Poi Pu Kai Hawaii on the island of Kauai. We stayed at the Villas of Poi Pu Kai in a luxurious penthouse villa – I saw one for sale on the internet in the same complex asking price $1.4M – we were in the lap of luxury. If I had a ranch styled home, this villa personifies how I would like it to look. Beautiful marble floor tiles, 4 bedrooms, 5 Bathroom, master bedroom suite with walk in closet, porcelain soak bathtub, walk in multi-head shower, his and her sink, private lanai. The kitchen had Kenmore, built in refrigerator, dishwasher, island with marble top, everything state-of-the-art. There was even a built in wall vacuum system. The open kitchen, dining room, living room with the huge walk-out lanai was the focal point of the villa. I bought enough food and drinks to wine and dine all of my guests for breakfast and dinner every day. I was the hostess with the mostest and they did not want for anything. One night after cooking one of my fantabulous meals, everyone had gone to bed, and my best friend had fallen asleep on the couch. I sat down in my Japanese Kimono that I had saved from my trip to Osaka for this occasion, and in the midst of the quiet I had the realization that if I did have a house like the villa it would not bring me happiness if I was unhappy.

I have worked hard for ungrateful employers; I have been in relationships that were not true representations of love. I have sacrificed myself to rear my children, and I have been looking for a mate, a miracle, a something that would save me and bring me happiness. But as simple and as cliché as this may sound, to be happy, you have to do the things that make you happy. And if you are anything like me, you have to break out of your mold of being everything for everybody, or just trying to rest so you can have a week of beating yourself up again in unloving situations, and dare to love yourself enough to change and to bring the focus on you – be selfish and unapologetic about it! Do things that make you laugh and smile and feel good. Be unconcerned with what other people, including friends and family think. Wear bright colored clothes that express who you are, regardless of whether the clothes are age appropriate or appropriate for you size. You are healthy, you are whole and you, dear heart, are here. In the infamous words of Beyoncé, "I was here, I lived, I loved" - you are here – live and love!!!! This is my prayer for you. Do not be afraid to be "the real you" dear hearts.

With Unapologetic Love,

Friday

PART 7

A SOUL AND SPIRIT UNSETTLED

Posted on August 4, 2012

"But somewhere in your mind's eye, you are saying, perhaps subliminally, that 'you are not good enough.' Behind that million-dollar confident look, and beautiful smile, is a soul and spirit that is unsettled. The flesh has ruled with the things that you thought would bring happiness, degrees, credentials, freedom; but as you stated, it is only a short lived emotion/feeling, bringing tears of sadness. You've embraced the sadness of your younger years where you did not have control. Instead you must learn how to embrace life from the endless possibilities."

The Therapist and I always go back and forth about astrology. I liken astrological characteristics to the Myers Briggs Personality Types. As a highly educated woman, she frowns at my comparison – but hey, astrology is my comfort zone, and I can relate traits easily from that perspective. The idea of subliminally thinking I am not good enough is very real for me – a Libran characteristic, and you guessed it, I am a Libra woman.

I have had enough occurrences in life when I have been 2nd place. With the 2012 Olympics going on right now there has been a tremendous amount of negative talk surrounding Michael Phelps coming in 2nd place and winning the silver medal. There is something about winning the gold that defines you as a true winner. Although for the record, Michael, you are a winner in my book, as is any other Olympian that wins medals. When I ran track, the fastest girl on our team was Darcell. I knew I could beat her and one day we raced and the finish line was literally a yard away. My legs were going so fast, I almost could not feel the floor, and in the moment that I had that thought, I tripped and fell to the ground. Darcell won the race and I was mad, and I told my mother I wanted to quit track after that race.

In high-school, there was a program in New York called New York Kids on Stage. This is another program that I had talked myself into. The program was supposed to give kids the opportunity to do Shakespeare in Central Park over the summer. The Director of the program that year was some highly sought after director and I was amped. About a week or two into the program he resigned to go work for Bill Cosby on The Cosby Show. Our summer in Central Park became a presentation for our parents in our practice space. My heart kind of turned on acting after that.

After moving to Los Angeles, I applied for Survivor the 6th Season. I shot an amazing submission video. My application was strong and intriguing and I got the call for a taped audition. I went to the audition, I had been working out, so I looked good, especially on camera. The interview audition was light and airy and funny. I got the call asking me to get a passport because I was on standby – and then I didn't make the cut. Just last year I applied to LAAAWPPI – Los Angeles African American Women Public Policy Institute, a wonderful organization that "creates a pipeline for women to assume leadership roles at all levels of government and public affairs." The richness of the stories of my life are motivators and the application that I submitted to this program was one of the strongest. My life passions were worn on my sleeves and the things legislatively I wanted to change were all the result of things that had happened to me, I poured the details into my application – and yet it was not good enough. I was invited to be the first alternate to the program, should any of the accepted applicants decline their acceptance. 2nd Place!

My uncle, God bless his heart, read my blog and it disturbed him to the point where he could not sleep. There was so much about this niece of his that he has been around since she was born, yet he did not really know some of the darkest secrets of her life. I told him today that I felt like I had hit a wall. I have been carrying so much for so long, including this notion of not being good enough, that I had to go through this process in order to express, to get it all out so that the weight of it all, could no longer hold me back. The burdens of survival were becoming too heavy. I want to be a winner at this game called life.

When I graduated from Howard University it was one of the proudest moments of my life. I knew since junior high school that Howard was where I wanted to go to college. When my guidance counselor in high school recommended I go to Brown, I told her I was going to Howard. In defiance I applied to the Business School and the Fine Arts School at Howard, and to Spellman. I did not apply to any other colleges. I got into both Howard and Spellman. When my high school boyfriend asked me what was going to happen to us when I went to college, I told him I really did not know, because that was the experience I wanted to have. Yet my life plan at that point seemed to expire.

Mentorship is very important. Have someone with experience coaching you through life professionally and personally. Surround yourself with people that have had the types of life experiences that you want to have. Let them talk to you about their failures and their triumphs which led to where they are. Let them reinforce the notion that you are good enough, smart enough, strong enough until that subliminal notion of not being good enough within you is expelled and so that new seeds are planted in you allowing you to eventually grow from within. I have said repeatedly to various friends and young people that not having a mentor was a huge handicap, especially professionally.

What is funny is that people have told me, men in particular, that I come off too strong. I am very direct and it can make people at times feel like they have to "step to me in a certain kind of way." Well that is true. Do not come to me half- assed in business or personally. Step to me "correctly." Know what you want and state it plainly. The intentions of people have not always been clear in my life and if you cannot state what you want plainly, then that is cause for me to look at you sideways.

My soul and spirit have been unsettled for many many moons. I have been waiting to be heard. I have been wanting to be loved. I have wanted to feel safe in this world. And I grew tired with the passage of time, my search was becoming unyielding. I felt myself losing control. Writing this blog has been one of the best things that I have done for myself and my spirit is happy. The word unapologetic seems to go against how we are socialized. You are supposed to apologize for not sharing, for saying something mean, for expressing yourself. Know your position, do not step out of line. My goodness I understand why old people are cranky. When your bones hurt you don't give a damn and you say what you want to say. But now imagine if your heart is hardened because over time you have suppressed your hurts, because you towed the line in silent agony. Now imagine if bitterness had consumed your very soul. Or imagine a psychotic episode that literally causes a split in your personality, because the weight of your sadness is so deep. I did not want that to be my reality, depression was setting in on me, and I knew it. I had to do something different to free my soul.

I want to soar like a mighty hawk in the sky. Be encouraged in where you are in life. "Embrace life from the endless possibilities." My uncle called me a "super human being" today. He used to call me the black cat because I seemed to always land on my feet. Until today, he had no idea of how many lives I had survived. For me right now, there is a certain uncertainty with my business; but for the first time in a long time, the pressure of having to succeed is gone, the idea of "I must get it right to be a success" is inaccuracy at its best. My spirit is soaring and embracing the infinite possibilities. I am successful because I dared to step out on faith – and that is indeed good enough!

Unapologetically,

Friday

PART 8

THE FORGIVENESS LETTER

Posted on August 5, 2012

"The forgiveness first comes with you forgiving little Friday. By telling her in a letter how proud you the adult Friday is for little Friday staying strong and surviving. She survived Friday, and she survived with amazing skill. Little Friday came through this experience helping the adult Friday to develop a heart to serve and help others."

This assignment came with some emotional releasing. I am proud of myself for many things. This exercise, however, requires me to connect to my inner child. I do not know if this will make sense; but within me, I guard her and protect her. This morning I went to my picture box and pulled out various things. I pulled out a school photo of me from the 2nd or 3rd grade, I am wearing a white shirt with a bow tie and a red dress with straps, I have on glasses and earrings and there is a silhouette without glasses. I sat with this photo and cried and held it close to my heart. Then I thought, if this child came to me with her story, I would want to give her a bath to wash away her sorrow and wrap her in a blanket, sit her on my lap, hug her and tell her it would all be alright. We would sit and rock in silence and I would simply be there for her. So I took a shower, put on my waffle robe, sat on the couch with my granny blanket and started this blog entry.

I sent The Actor a text that said "As I look at this picture of me from the 2nd or 3rd grade, I almost cannot be believe my own life. And I wonder why in the world would anyone want to violate her…" I am a beautiful little girl, who as a child received very mixed messages: you are an ugly 4 eyes but you are wanted for the sexual gratification of others. I am saddened and angry that these are the messages that I received.

Dear Little Friday,

You indeed were a beautiful little girl with a happy disposition and I love you. You were able to manage an impossible situation of living in a home with domestic violence and you did as you were asked by your mother, you kept her secrets. You sacrificed yourself and allowed your mother's abuser to use you for his sexual pleasure and you kept his secret because he threatened to kill your mother. You were a child and you should never have been asked to keep these secrets. But you did, and despite your tired days of being at school, and maintaining the appearance of normalcy in a less than normal situation, you went to school and you excelled intellectually. You were one of the smartest girls in the 2nd grade. You could read above grade level, and you were smart enough to be skipped to the third grade, despite your mother holding you back. You were a brilliant little girl and I am proud of you.

During your two-year stint in Virginia, you must have worn your love for your mother on your sleeves. But then she was gone long enough where people could see your longing for her in your eyes. When your child uncle and his cousin constantly touched your private parts and told you if you did not let them, they would tell your mother, as if you had done something wrong, I am here to tell you little girl that you had done nothing wrong. Those little boys were wrong, and someone had planted a toxic seed within them, that made them think they, as boys, should have their way with girls, even if it meant threatening girls and being liars. Your teen uncle attempted to rape you in the same house that your stepfather had visited and violated you in. It's the same house where the child uncle and his friend kicked in a bathroom door just to see your nakedness. There were so many people in that home, and no one saw you and yet you survived. Even though you felt unprotected in your very skin, know that I love you and know that you are safe, and you are a whole being.

When you returned to Brooklyn and found yourself at PS 262, yet again in a hostile environment. You managed the best you could. When the mean girl bullies chased you home, you ran just to survive. When you were tired of running, you stood your ground, not knowing if you really knew how to fight, but you were again violated and angry enough that you made it clear to the girl who the mean girls presented in front of you that you did not want to fight, but you were also not going to run and she had a choice to make. Despite this, you again excelled in school and were accepted to a magnet school. I am proud of you for standing up for yourself. You were again in a situation where someone should have protected you, but you knew that no one would, so you protected yourself. Do you know how strong you are?

You developed a curvaceous body at the age of ten and every boy in middle school seemed to notice. You endured inappropriate touches on the play yard that you had learned were something to not be told. And you still excelled. You auditioned in school plays because you wanted to act and you did your best. You received awards in computers, music and science. When you were faced with a boy you liked, you again were placed in an impossible situation by being told if you came home pregnant you would be kicked out. You were not told what questions to ask yourself to see if you were really ready for sex, and you were not emotionally. You were not provided a safe environment to express yourself without being judged. You were not told that sex should be a wonderful experience and that your pleasure was primary. You were not even talked to about birth control, so that if you decided to have sex, you could protect yourself from pregnancy and std's. You had sex with this boy and after ten months of being his girlfriend, when you thought you might be pregnant, he avoided you and then broke up with you, leaving you feeling abandoned. There was no one in your life to help you manage your emotions, and I forgive you for the choices you made.

You went on to high school and you started finding your own voice and your own identity. There were other smart kids at school to enjoy. You danced in talent shows. You learned the importance of voting from Mr. Mott, Martin Luther King's nephew. You worked in retail and developed your own sense of style. You represented your high school in Washington DC and on a scholastic television show. You were the friend that the pregnant girls could confide in, whichever way they decided to choose. You talked one of your friends through the night she wanted to take her life. You got yourself to college Friday.

In college you made some of the best friendships. Even though The College BF led to heartbreak, you also experienced what it was like to give unconditional love. You had children too young rebounding from your heartbreak, but you are a good mom, Friday. Without the help of their father, you have given your children unforgettable experiences, from slow beach days, to Sea World, to trips to Mexico, Los Vegas, New York, Philadelphia, Washington DC, and Hawaii. You made sure they saw their Great-great-grandmother before she passed away. When your son was born a preemie, and had a day where it seemed he might die, you based on the records that you kept on his feeding schedules, you were able to identify the problem to the doctors, and they changed his feeding schedule so that it would be less stressful on his body, when he had open heart surgery you did not waver or fall apart like so many other mothers, you knew he would be fine. You provided a protected environment for your children, so that they would not have your life experiences; you talk to them openly about sex and their emotions, letting them know that they truly can come to you about anything; you worked tirelessly to keep a roof over their heads, and you tried your best to keep them in the same school district from kindergarten through high school to provide them with the sense of stability that you did not feel you had. You chose to leave their father immediately after he demonstrated that he could be abusive. When you saw that your son had special educational needs that required different learning environments, you became his advocate. You did not let a label become an excuse, you challenged him and provided the learning environments and tutoring as best as you could afford in order to give him the opportunity to learn and excel with confidence. When your children tell you that they want to be something or try something, if it is within your means, you give them those experiences and support them, and even when their loves and wants are outside of your means, you tell them not to let your limitations be an excuse for them not to follow their dreams. Friday, you have raised confident, articulate, beautiful children; you are at times the unconventional, outspoken, yet quintessential mother.

Thanks to you Little Friday, I have a compassionate heart that speaks especially to the needs of women and children. I have hosted fundraisers for One by One – an exceptional organization that provides surgical repairs to obstetric fistula caused by unrelieved obstructed labor in women and young girls in developing nations. I have hosted a fundraiser for ANSA – Artists for a New South Africa, I have helped contribute to the purchase of a goat for a family in Haiti, I volunteer with the Snoop Youth Football League – Crenshaw Colts Chapter – because I am compelled to support women and girls based on all that I know can and does happen to them. I am you, Little Friday.

You are so courageous that when your employers could no longer offer you a purpose for your working for them, other than to be used as a human asset as they wanted, you left and started your own business management practice during an economic recession. Based on choices that you made, you own your home, investment property, and beachfront property that will one day be a great vacation villa. You are a lady that in her best year made $63K and yet you somehow have accomplished so much more material success than you give yourself credit for. You are amazing, Friday! And you are a success because of your courage.

And now, as you take this time to know yourself better, because up until now, you have had to be so many things for so many people, remember that it is okay to say no. It is okay to disappoint another person, if you are doing what you need to do for yourself first. Other people will step in to fill those gaps. The people that can rock with you will and it is okay for some people to fall to the side. Allow yourself time, time to feel, time to forgive, and time to discover. You are a beautiful human being, and you deserve a good life, to be treated with love and respect and kindness. You are a true American Shero!

With Unapologetic Love,

Friday

THE ROAD TO FORGIVENESS

And when the sun's rays hit her face, the healing had begun.

The Real Friday Jones

PART 1

CONTEMPLATION

Posted on August 8, 2012

The Forgiveness Letter was a challenge. Reflecting on my life when looked at it in its entirety is quite the feat. I read childhood diaries. I was astonished to find that the boy I lost my virginity to broke up with me after ten months when my period was late. According to my diary entry, he was "bored." Ironically, boredom set in after I thought I might be pregnant. It seems men have the issues and mental capacity of teenage boys. Luckily I was not pregnant, but the very next boy I dated received a two-page questionnaire, which I also found folded up in my childhood diary. And I have been grilling guys, asking questions, trying to gauge is this relationship one where I have the least likelihood of being hurt. Can I ask enough questions on the front end to determine if this guy is honest and honorable and most importantly capable of love? Can this guy love me – I have asked every man that I dated some variation of these questions, ill prepared myself to fully commit emotionally – but hoping that I might one day decipher their truth, their true intentions, before I give them all of me. Well, my method although it's logical, it is not scientific and the results have been abysmal at best. Generally, people do not reveal who they really are until 6 months or 12 months of knowing you – in the beginning the representative shows up. My representative, however, is generally the same at day one as it is at day 365. However, my truth is that my representative is the adult me allowing only the purest of heart to see the inner child in me, almost like a Disney movie, waiting for Prince Charming to kiss me as I was Snow White, bringing me back to life.

The Therapist

Every time I read your entries I'm humbled by all that you've shared. It's amazing to me just how much you've held in over the years and have still managed to do and accomplish all that you have. The speed at which you are finally processing all these emotions lets me know you are ready to cleanse for once and for all. Thank you for sharing.

These thoughts have dominated your way of being, all of your life. You know no other way of self-expression, other than the defensive style that was developed by Little Ms. Friday. Now you must let her know you (the adult Ms. Friday) is ready to lead.

Your letter was very comprehensive. I felt the love and regard you have for Ms. F. Have you said everything you wanted to express? Take a few days to reflect in that space?

It's important that you let her cleanse all of that part of her life for once and for all. Then, you need her to know that You are fully available to protect her, and the mean people are all gone. This integration will start to unfold when you express to her that in order for you to mature and grow, you need to forgive and release all of the mean people that have hurt her. You need to also forgive and release your mom. After all, her lack of parenting skills exposed you to a very damaging abusive childhood.

I'm not sure what would be the right way for you to do this for you are very close with your mother right now. You might feel better writing a letting of forgiveness instead of face to face. What you are basically reconciling is all the things she didn't give you and the pain that has caused you to learn and protect yourself during your primary years. You still have anger and bitterness there, similarly to all of the folks who violated you. She was a part of that violation that you must acknowledge. So writing, not in an open blog, may be the best way you can get that emotion out.

Forgiveness is a slow process, because you must acknowledge the pain of all the people who have hurt you and then let it go. Some people have written the pain of their past down and then piece by piece have had a fire pit party, letting the memories of their past burn to ashes for once and for all. Yours may be the culmination of writing your book and helping others. The point is whatever way of release that works for you, it is like you're coming out party, letting those memories of your past know "they" cannot hurt or control your emotions anymore. You're announcing you're no longer going to be a victim of their evil ways, particularly in your mind. Forgiveness is a willful process.

Once that is complete, you should be emotionally free to start re-narrating the true essence of who the adult Ms. Friday is. What spiritually guides you? What do you think your journey was all about? And your presence fulfills what purpose?

You have come a long way Ms. Friday in a very short time. Appreciate you. Love who you are and the strength that you have. If you've accomplished all that you have under such distressful circumstance, I can't wait to see what you'll accomplish after this process.

Ms. Friday, be slow in the forgiveness process. You really need to get to a good place in that. For once the forgiveness process is complete, you're free to create and grow without any old baggage holding you back. Most of the process is asking yourself: Are you ready to forgive and be free to move on? Have you cried your last tear? Can you use the pain from the past as a source of future strength? Can you forgive you for all the knucklehead relationships you had that didn't help you define you? Can you define what forgiveness is for you?

Take your time Ms. Friday, breathe and appreciate life and the journey along the way.

Now if you have been following, you will recall that I sent The Actor a text. He really does know how to talk to my soul. In his playful self "you were a cute child. What happened?" anticipating my smile, which is one of his favorite things "Oh, you just got even better looking." And then his soothing words, "Nothing is irreparable… sometimes we must go back in time to repair things in our mind and soul. That makes the future a much happier place, and if we can find forgiveness in our hearts, even better. One thing I have found is that at one point or another in our tormentor's life, he or she was themselves tormented. It doesn't fix what's happened, but it does help to humanize the individual. Let little Friday know she is loved. You know why? She is."

Words of wisdom! I did take about two days to sit with myself, in different quiet moments. Had I said everything that I wanted to say in my letter? Not exactly. I also wanted to forgive myself for wanting a home so badly, that I at one point was willing to settle for something less than love. You may ask, *how could someone that has been searching for love since her teenage years decide to settle?* – I thought it would bring me happiness and contentment. I had to stop and ask the questions: who am I, what am I chasing, and why?

Unapologetically,

Friday

PART 2

FORGIVING AN OUTLIER

Posted on August 9, 2012

The predatory behaviors of men around the world seems to be acceptable and the domination of women the norm. As far-fetched as this may seem, forgiving my violators, would also require me to find a way to forgive "QRS." When the grainy tape surfaced with the "alleged" thirteen-year-old child, a friend asked me if I wanted to see it. I told them no. They said you have to see it, there is no way he can say it's not him, they put the video on pause so I could see the man in the video. What stuck in my mind from the still was the width of the man's hands across this child's back. I was immediately sickened. And a fan had been lost.

When you are undeniably talented, it is as if society will forgive the predatory behaviors of men. There is something wrong with a little bump and grind when you are "allegedly" a grown-assed man pissing and having sex with an "alleged" thirteen-year-old child. It disgusted me that his fans purchased the works of the Outlier in droves. The conversation around the neighborhood, particularly from women was: that girl was a gold digger, she must have wanted it, or she lied to him. This vilification of this female child incensed me – it was as if an adult male was not responsible for his alleged actions. These are probably the same mothers that baby their boys and do not hold their sons accountable for their actions. My question for these women would always be at thirteen, so what if she was or had done any of those things? Between the Outlier being famous and having means, he was the adult, and as the adult he wielded the most authority and power in that predatory relationship. At thirteen-years-old – a child has practically zero earning potential and a lot of big eyed wants, based on how we are socialized to be consumers; so again, so what if she was socialized to want things including money and was a "gold digger?" And if this child did want to have sex with this man – there is a host of possible reasons, all leading to some kind of lack in her life: lack of resources aka money, lack of nice name brand clothes and shoes, lack of food at home, lack of self-esteem, lack of self-love, lack of parental love, lack of life direction, etc. I was one of those girls that developed at age ten, so her looking mature for her age is in no way something new under the sun. It does not give grown men license to be having sex with you because you look ready. If you're being physically ready is the only consideration from a man, then he is viewing you as an object to be used for his sexual gratification only – the kind of man that will nut, and not put in the work to make sure you are satisfied. There were plenty of times while walking to the corner store, that I could see grown-assed men with their mouths open as if the water was gathering like a salivating dog; and I would look them in the eye and say – stop looking at me, you are old enough to be my father. That would shame most of them to turn away, and for the twisted men, I remember an occasional smile as if they relished in the idea and they would continue to look at me. A grown man should not have been "allegedly" fucking any child, at thirty-five years old. So, the question is can I forgive my violators, and can I forgive an Outlier? And to be honest – I did try last year. I was driving in my car listening to "Love Letters," but I remember thinking…. did you write this song with a grown woman in mind or a teenage girl – the image of kids passing notes in class came to my mind. The image lingered just a little too long… and I changed the station.

The Therapist:

It's important that you cleanse all of that part of your life for once and for all. You need to forgive and release all of the mean people that have hurt you. You need to forgive and release your mom. "Most of the process is asking yourself, are you ready to forgive and be free to move on. Have you cried your last tear? Can you use the pain from the past as a source of future strength? Can you forgive you for all the knucklehead relationships you had that didn't help you define you? Can you define what forgiveness is for you?"

The looming questions are: Am I truly ready to forgive these people in my life that have so powerfully affected me, and can I define what forgiveness means in relation to me? I am ready to forgive these people, because I must. I have been carrying the emotional baggage around for far too long, and there is so much more that I want to do, I can no longer let the weight of all these emotions slow me from what it is that I need to do now. I need strength, and you cannot be strong and stable if you are riding an emotional roller coaster every other day. If I can manage to articulate what forgiveness means for each of these people as it relates to me, I will have a fairly decent shot. The Actor recommended humanizing the tormentor – he found often that his tormentors were tormented, the violators were once violated. I must consider this, as there is no way I can hold on to the anger in even the smallest amount and be free emotionally, I will have to find a way to forgive each person entirely.

Oftentimes I have to let my emotions rest with me when I do not feel quite right about a situation or event. I have to let my emotions develop into words. Usually once I can articulate how I truly feel about something – I can let it go once expressed and I can make peace with a situation or an individual. It seems like if I can do that here, including with the big enchilada that is my mother, I will have a fairly good shot at moving on once and for all. That sounds exciting and I hope that for anyone reading this, who may have had similar life experiences, you can ask yourself these tough questions, and develop the answers that are most appropriate for you. Only you know. Just remember, be kind to yourself through this process. Love yourself through this process. And if you have to experience feelings that you would rather continue to hide and bury, allow those feelings to well up – cry, yell, laugh, write, whatever – but get it all out, and let it all go once and for all.

Unapologetically,

Friday

PART 3

A KEY TO LIFE

Posted on August 13, 2012

You can always tell when I am wrestling a bit with the subject matter – my posts are usually a couple of days apart in those instances. Yesterday I helped to celebrate one of my newest friend's birthday. She lives in a beautiful Downtown Los Angeles high-rise apartment building, with a rooftop pool deck that could shame some 5-star hotels. There are stunning views of Los Angeles, cabanas, high end cooking ranges, and an infinity styled pool. She was celebrating her 40th Birthday. What I love about her is when she dances, she is chock full of energy and her smile radiates like she is at the happiest place on earth.

I thought about my 40th Birthday which I spent with close friends and family. I thought about who was in the room to celebrate life and I felt overwhelmed by the fact that these people loved me enough to celebrate my life. Then I thought about one of my dear friends who lost a niece to suicide. Her story made local headlines in Los Angeles because the niece was a local celebrity with a fledgling singing career, and she had done vocals on a couple of rap albums. This girl was 24-years-old and beautiful. She reminded me of my youngest sister, light-skinned, head full of hair, chiseled cheek bones – beautiful. At some point when I was on the swanky pool deck, I walked to the edge and looked over, you could see down to the ground. This beautiful young girl with her life ahead of her had jumped from a radio tower to her death. I turned around to look at everyone on the pool deck and I thought in the moment that she jumped, she basically said goodbye to all of the people that loved her. Then I thought how much pain she must have been in to make such a final decision. Who did she need to forgive, including herself? What was so terrible that she could not forgive? And what was so heavy that she decided to leave the planet earth forever and everyone that loved her?

I was ready to forgive – everyone.

This morning at 7:18 AM I lit a candle for the tormented soul that is/ was my step-father. I did not like his energy from day one. I thank the universe for heightening my instincts and allowing me now as an adult to see people for who they are and how they are, not how I might want them to be. LT I forgive you for entering my family's life and inflicting fear and control over us – emotions that you must have been yourself struggling with, particularly a lack of control in your own life. I forgive you for making alcohol your companion of choice rather than spending time with yourself to actually deal with your personal demons. I forgive you for the many times that you physically abused my first love, leaving her to hide her shame with make-up and sunglasses. I forgive you for making sure fear was so well instilled in me that I was afraid that you might kill any one of my family members at your will. I forgive you for showing me Playboy magazines and introducing the idea that sex was a game to be kept secret. I forgive you for teaching me at an early age that sex was for the gratification of men, and that my body and soul were simply to be used. I forgive you for tying the negative emotion of fear with sex. I forgive you for arousing my body when I was not ready, and in such a way where I was uncomfortable with sex and my own body for years to come. I forgive you for every time you laid me down or woke me up to violate me. I forgive you because you know not what you do.

I choose life and to celebrate life with great joy. I choose to be fearless and to love every inch of myself, from head to toe. I choose Me and the world will hear my voice and I will hold my head up high because I chose life.

With tears in the wells of my eyes, I am blowing out the candle, and as the rings of smoke circle, I inhale, and exhale and let this go....

Unapologetically,

Friday

PART 4

THE VIRGINIANS

Posted on August 15, 2012

You know I am still amazed that there are two years of my school life that are completely blocked out of my memory. I often tell people that when it comes to time, I am not good at remembering how long ago something happened or what age I was when something happened. I have to think really hard to come within the ball-park, and I think this may be why. When you drink too much and black out – which I have done twice in this lifetime, once in high school and once in college - you kind of know there was a fairly simple reason, you drank too much. When you are a child and you black out, not for one night, but for two years of a very specific part of your life, there too is a reason, except it is a little complicated – there is a deep need to protect yourself.

The Family that I have in Virginia is pretty much a non-factor in my life. As an adult, I do not visit, I have no desire to visit, and I certainly have no desire for my children to get to know them, based on the simple premise that "they are family." Just because people are family does not mean that you have to have them in your life. At some point you choose the people you want in your life, including your family. I truly am blessed in that I have some of the best friends, ever, and I love being with them. The

Virginians, perhaps they are good people, but for me, distance has been good and time coupled with space makes it a little easier to forgive.

I forgive the teachers and the school environment that existed for me in the 3rd and 4th grades. I forgive you because the environment was so hostile, that I can only recall one day at school – the day my mother was called because I was thought to be retarded. I forgive you for being unable to recognize intelligence in a little black girl. I forgive you for not knowing how to relate to a gifted child. I forgive you for not engaging intelligence and allowing for a child in your presence to be invisible.

I have been very careful not to name names and this is a time when I wish I could, but I will maintain the level of integrity that I have developed through this process. For the Uncle and Cousin that were about my age DA and TA I forgive you. You were boys. The notion of entitlement seemed to be part of your upbringing. Your parents and the people in your life were responsible for teaching you that women and girls are sacred, and they did not. You were taught that girls were to be exploited, you were taught that your curiosity about the female body outweighed the level of respect that you were to have for a female's body, you were taught that touching a girl's vagina and seeing a girl's nakedness did not require her permission, you were taught to violate girls. So I forgive you, your parents, and the other influencers in your life that taught you these things were okay because you were boys. DA you are dead now and your mother had to clean your room, in all of its disorder, including all of the condoms that were strewn about, I remember the tears she shed for you when she had to bury you, the youngest of her sons. I hope that should you return to life for another human experience, that you will return with a higher regard for girls and women.

For my Teenage Uncle. GA I forgive you for the infamous day you were left alone with me, lacking babysitting skills. I forgive you for thinking it was okay to strip a child naked and to lay on top of her humping her for your sexual gratification and only stopping because adults returned to the house unexpectedly. I forgive you because it was one day of misjudgment by you that has stayed with me for all of the days of my life. You also grew up with your brother DA who you were very jealous of, to the same parents that did not teach you that women and girls were sacred. You were also taught that girls were to be exploited, and for you that translated into obtaining your own sexual gratification by force was okay. I forgive you because once you were a man, and I had confessed your attempted rape to your father – my grandfather - at the family reunion. When confronted with the fact that I did remember, and I had outed you because your wife was pregnant with a female child, you were not man enough to admit the truth. I forgive you for calling me during our family reunion to explain to me how I must have been confused, yet you remember the exact day according to you that "you were supposed to give me a shower." I forgive you for calling my mother almost 14 or 15 years after the fact in an attempt to speak with me again to help me remember, as if my memory is somehow unclear, and for continuing to deny the truth. I forgive you because you are ill-equipped to be honest with yourself and you are a grown man.

I forgive the boy that lived across the street "R." I remember him as being a good kid. Unfortunately, I remember the day my child Uncle went across the street to go get him while I was taking a bath and the two of them kicking the door in to see my nakedness. "R", I forgive you for being a juvenile boy who thought that this behavior was acceptable. I forgive you for seeing my nakedness and laughing and running away, leaving me feeling embarrassed and ashamed of my body, and leaving me feeling violated. I forgive you because you may remember that day or have long forgotten about it. I forgive you because I will never know.

I have been called tough. Even The Therapist has said I am guarded and I have "heightened" sensitivities to certain things. With this life that I have had, how could I not be guarded or have "normal" sensitivities – I learned at a very young age, at 6 and 7 years old to be very guarded, to protect myself. I honestly am amazed that I am even interested in the opposite sex. The predatory behavior of men saddens me. I see my strength; it is quiet but always present. I envy daddies' girls. Those girls that grew up protected with their dad's wrapped around their fingers. There is a softness that they as women have, that I do not have. They know how to be tender with a man, and I in contrast am direct – I have even been told that I act like a man emotionally. It is as if I have lost some of my femininity at the hands of men and boys.

Unapologetically,

Friday

PART 5

WHEN IT'S IMPORTANT

Posted on August 16, 2012

This is actually not part of my therapy – This is just the reality of my day.

I woke up this morning feeling good – I had an amazing dream that The Actor had a home with folding walls – his home. He had prepared a superb dinner and I was walking in his home to the kitchen with an empty plate in my hand, but I was unsure of which way to go. He opened the wall separating the bedroom from the kitchen and asked, let me get that for you. He took my empty plate to the sink and said "I got you." I woke up feeling taken care of, feeling like there was no real distance between us.

But yesterday, I gave notice ending the month to month lease at my office. My partner and I had to figure out what was needed to work remotely from our respective homes, I had the reality that I will have to find a job in order for my family to survive. I dared to dream….

Today the client that left my long term employer in my Jerry Maguire moment along with me told me over lunch that she and her husband could no longer afford my services. By 2:00 PM today I was writing The Actor a letter responding to what I believe was an ultimatum and I chose me – I told him I hoped his interest in me was enough for him to come back to the table with possible changes that he was willing to make – a compromise – but I have to accept the fact that he may not come back to the table at all…

Thank god I have a roof over my head, I have my health and my children have theirs – but this was just one day.

I am at the bottom and I hope the universe has a plan, because I tried and I have cried my last cry, I have nothing left but to survive. But I guess that is what I do.

I wonder if this is when miracles happen…

Friday

PART 6

MEAN PEOPLE

Posted on August 17, 2012

Perhaps we were the generation that bullied. I have two children - both in public schools. Every year at the beginning of school I have to sign school rules documents with all kinds of anti-bullying and zero tolerance for sexual harassment and fighting. Progress. Kids can be mean – the "Nelsons" on the school yard that take Bart Simpson's lunch money are not always boys from broken down homes – sometimes they are girls.

Up to the 2nd grade, I would say I lived a pretty happy and normal life – for me it was an enchanted life. But as you know, second grade is when things changed both at school and at home. My second grade teacher was a short mean Jewish teacher. The way I learned I think annoyed this woman to no end. As a child I tended to process information verbally. Even now, sometimes when I am working through something in my head, I talk out loud. At my old job, people learned to ignore me, my babbling out loud did not necessarily mean I was talking to anybody. This woman, despite her being Jewish, would have fit in perfectly as a mean nun at a Catholic School. Silence seemed to be golden – and I was far from silent. Between being smart enough to finish work before my classmates and actually talking to my friends and babbling through actual class work – I am sure that I was quite the chatty Kathy, and it drove my second grade teacher nuts.

So Miss S, from Public School 137, I forgive you for not being able to manage the way I learned. I forgive you for snapping on stage during rehearsal for our class play when you told us not to run off stage. Despite the fact that every child had run off stage before me, I forgive you for grabbing me by my neck and lifting me up on the wall while choking me to tell me – do not run off stage. I forgive you for making me cry and seeing you for the mean teacher that you were. I forgive you for not knowing how to deal with a child in the second grade that read at the fifth grade level. I forgive you – you were really just an angry woman who wanted children to be seen not heard.

Now this odd lot of fifth grade girls, were all big girls, -womanly type of girls that I guess I should be able to relate to, as puberty hit them in the fifth grade one year before me, and they must have been awkward in their bodies. Imagine what a full figured Tocarra Jones may have looked like in the fifth grade – now imagine that she was mean and not so pretty, and had four friends in her little clique that physically looked just like her – and imagine that they were all mean too. Well that is exactly what I was dealing with at Public School 262 in the fifth Grade. This little crew of haters hated everything about me, from the way I dressed, to my not so Brooklyn southern accent; from my two-year stint in Virginia, to how smart I was. According to them I came out of nowhere and took over as teacher's pet, replacing the smart girl they already had in class. This mean bunch of girls literally chased me home every day. And again, even though I knew they were wrong – I really did not know how to tell somebody. The crazy part is the ring leader of this bunch had two fingers on her left hand. I remember thinking how the heck could you be mean when you are physically disabled – you only have two damn fingers. But reality is all of these girls had probably been teased for everything from being tall, having breasts; and I am sure the girl with two fingers had heard more commentary than my being 4-eyed because kids are mean.

So to this fifth Grade clique of mean girls from PS 262 – I forgive you. I forgive you for being so uncomfortable with yourselves, that you did not know how to welcome a new kid to school. I forgive you for being jealous of my being smart, as if it somehow heightened your true school performance as being less than. I forgive you for chasing me home every day, and putting the nicest girl in your clique in front of me to fight on the day I decided I was not going to run any more. I forgive you for being so mean – you did not know how to show kindness. I forgive you for being so mean, that I became so defensive, that I even started to be mean to the people that had been nice to me.

The thing that I have learned is, even as an adult, there are mean people that you sometimes have to work with. They may bark orders or be just plain difficult to work with. You have to not take their actions personally, let them know what you will and will not tolerate in terms of communication, and figure out how to get the job done. But typically, like the Nelson character on The Simpsons there is a reason why children bully, and there is usually a reason why adults are mean. Just know it is not really your responsibility to find out or to try to resolve.

Unapologetically,

Friday

PART 7

KNUCKLEHEAD RELATIONSHIPS

Posted on August 20, 2012

"...letting those memories of your past know "they" cannot hurt or control your emotions anymore. You're announcing you're not longer going to be a victim of their evil ways, particularly in your mind. Forgiveness is a willful process. Most of the process is asking yourself are you ready to forgive and be free to move on. Have you cried your last tear? Can you use the pain from the past as a source of future strength? Can you forgive you for all the knuckle head relationships you had that didn't help you define you?"

Forgiving myself for knucklehead relationships.... hmmm. You know this Road to Self- Discovery has been very interesting. As I write and reflect on relationships, I realize that I have been broken since I was 13 years old. That is when I started liking boys, liking boys while at the same time not trusting men to the point of not wanting to be left alone with male family members. At thirteen, I had my first boyfriend and was dumped in ten months when he thought I was pregnant, according to him, because he was now bored. So now I started to not trust boys – leaving the boys who would grow into men - left to answer my relentless questions all so I could feel the emotions of trust and safety. Wanting to feel trust and safety so I could simply love. From six to thirteen, I had all of these experiences that said I cannot trust you, I am not safe with you, I have been abandoned and violated by you, and yet I still want to love you. Because if I can figure out how to love you, I can be the real me and find happiness. I have been trying to figure this puzzle out my entire life. I have been trying to reconcile being loved and being able to be me. But those concepts are so fragmented. $1+1=2$. Simple equation, but I have been with many men and my story has yet to end with me being part of a permanent 2. And now my therapist wants me to forgive myself for knuckleheaded relationships that did not help define me.

I do not know how to define me. I am quite the enigma. It actually saddens me that I am bold bad and kick ass. I negotiate tough as nails, I can analyze a business situation or come up with a creative business strategy for a film, but put me in a relationship with emotions where there are little facts and no numbers, and it all blurs. I am a grown woman trying to reconcile the fact that the world is not always a safe place, and these man boys may hurt you or lie or be unclear on if they want to be with you or not, and if it is one that you love and for me there was only one, you will accept all kinds of behaviors that violate your boundaries, redefining yourself to what you think he wants, only to be told you are not good enough. Yet I am left wanting to be me, wanting to express, wanting to see how I actually feel about you, because if I can feel myself within a relationship, then I can grow like there is no cap on the amount of love that I can experience – because I am a well that wants to give. The problem is I do not know how to win. I am just now coming into my own voice. In my youth I was ultra-defensive, I handed out more ultimatums – well if you do not like it, kick rocks. Never really let anyone in. Now I have lowered my guard, I do not know how to play the games that men and women play. I am raw emotions and open and just plain naive about some things. How does one forgive the relationships that reinforced fear, anxiety over loss? I do not even know how to reign my emotions in when I start feeling, I am a waterfall of emotion – how does one forgive this?

When you tell a child to say they are sorry, you can tell them what the appropriate response is or how to correct the situation. I do not know what the appropriate responses are within a relationship. I know how to keep trying when I should walk away. Even when I am not feeling someone, sometimes I linger trying to be fair about giving the poor souls a chance to redeem themselves. And mind you this also works with guys that love me religiously, doing anything for me, bearing gifts, and I am not feeling the sexual chemistry – even then I do not tap out – I analyze trying to understand why I do not love them as much as they love me. Sometimes wishing I could just settle and be happy while at the same time demanding more from life – demanding prince charming – perfection, even though I know it does not exist. How do you forgive that?

I can forgive all of the poor relationships I was in, I can forgive the times I was afraid and bolted too soon. I can forgive guys for loving me too much too fast and for not loving me enough. But I have no idea on how to forgive me, because I do not know the solution – how to fix it. When will I be vulnerable and be able to be me, tough in the boardroom and a softie at home; and be loved in the same way that I give – when will I be able to exhale?

I do not know if this is the response The Therapist envisioned. "Can I use the pain from my past as a source of future strength?" In this case I honestly do not know – how can you be strong in a game you do not know how to play? I want to move on but there is a part of me that does not even want to play anymore I am not very confident in relationships, in their sustainability and yet I hope with all of my heart that one day I might get it right so that 1+1=2, and I am part of a 2… and happy. But perhaps that is a delusion too.

Unapologetically,

Friday

PART 8

ACCEPTANCE

Posted on <u>August 23, 2012</u>

I can forgive all of the poor relationships I was in, I can forgive the times I was afraid and bolted too soon, I can forgive guys for loving me too much too fast and for not loving me enough. But I have no idea on how to forgive me, because I do not know the solution – how to fix it. When will I be vulnerable and be able to be me, tough in the boardroom and a softie at home and be loved in the same way that I give – when will I be able to exhale?

Yesterday's entry required a call from The Therapist…and a cool glass of lemon verbena mint tea over ice. Make an 8oz glass of your favorite lemon verbena tea – sweeten to taste. Take about four to six mint leaves and place in a blender with 5-6 cubes of ice – crush the ice. Pour sweetened tea over the ice – and have a glass.

The Therapist

"Miss Friday – you should write a book. There are so many women that have gone through similar situations and feel exactly the way you do."

Now I did rehash a lot of what was in my last blog entry with The Therapist. As I explained my inability to forgive something I could not resolve or fix, I thought about my children. I have a son 17 and a daughter 14. Because of my life experiences there have been very conscious choices as to how I would raise them. I have made the point, with both of my children to say, "you are handsome son and daughter you are beautiful – know that for yourself. Do not let the fact that a girl or boy that you like tell you that you are good looking and then you act like it is not something you already know – accept the compliment. If that is all someone can find to like about you – move on." I have also told them that if they find as they start dating, that they really like someone, that is when they should stop and observe things like: does the person say something and then follow through with their actions, are they consistent in how they deal with you or do they run hot and cold, are they a good friend? I have also told both of them, "do not let someone manipulate you because they know that you have feelings for them, know that they have feelings for you too." As a mother I can enable my kids with tools to manage their emotions – however I am ill equipped to handle my emotions because I was never given adequate tools by my mother. I understand what all of this is logically, but I do not know it, and when I am in the thick of a relationship, finding balance is very difficult. My kids know what to do, simply because I told them what to do – no one ever guided me as to what to do within relationships and so I do not know what to do.

The Therapist said – *WOW*.

I asked what exercises or tools did she have for me because I understand my issues – but there still is the 'how do I forgive myself'– because I still do not know how to fix it. The Therapist said she would think on that and get back to me with something else – perhaps an action word other than forgive. What I resolved was "acceptance." Sometimes there is no solution, life is not always fair, bad things happen to good people and through it all you still have to love yourself. And I do love me, and I accept my life experiences as they happened, and I accept that I do not really know how to be in a relationship. I also accept that when I allow myself to be vulnerable, I am an overflowing well of emotions wanting to pour out an abundance of love that for decades I have been waiting to express. I accept the good, the bad, and the ugly. I accept me as I am, and I am so proud of myself for wanting to understand me better.

I spoke to my brother this morning. He returned from a tour in Asia. Personally I am challenged right now, my business is not self-sustaining, my car needs some repairs that will be costly, there is a list of things my children need, I need to re-enter the work force to get my family and business on track, and The Actor has to follow his joys and his life's joy, which right now requires all of his attention and I still love him dearly because he has touched the depth of my soul and I am forever changed – but this seems to be our reality, and I am an independent mom with bills and pressure. My stress level is off the Richter scale. In talking to my brother about life and my relationships and being defensive versus the complete opposite, which for me is a vulnerable well of emotions and the idea that I consider myself to be consistently me. I feel like I do not send a representative on dates. I am open and easy going, I do not tend to change – what you see is what you get. But the reality is I have been defensive within most of my relationships. My brother said "if you learned how to be defensive then who are you?" I said I do not know. My brother hit the nail on the head, that is exactly what I am trying to figure out through this process. When you start to understand where some of your behaviors come from, how some of your responses to people and events are learned behaviors to protect yourself from some point in your life when you should have been protected but were not – it is then that you can begin to see yourself. It is then that you can start having more understanding with yourself so that you come through, not as the wounded child within, not some replication of your parents, or a reflection of ingrained religion or societal roles placed upon you, but you.

When I wrote the "The Issues Part 2- Fear of Telling" chapter, I had an epiphany. I consider myself fairly quiet during sex. I have talked to girlfriends and they are like girl, you have never just screamed or said some obscene dirty ish…. and I will usually smile or chuckle – no. They are amazed – I am considered the outspoken one but yet I feel like I filter all the time. When I was six, I had secrets to keep for my abuser, and I had to protect my mother's very life with my quiet; then I was threatened and told to be quiet by the two uncles and their incestuous behavior. When I was a teen, sex was a sin and I was going to hell for fornicating, so I had to sneak to have sex and be quiet. When I had my first "O" it was *be quiet so my parents do not hear you.* Somewhere through the process it had been drilled into me to be quiet about sex. It was dirty, it was a secret, it was for sinners or bad girls. Sex is an amazingly beautiful experience and I will have an opportunity to get all of these restraints and conditioned behaviors out of my head and have an earth shattering "O" that might make me howl to the moon. I cannot wait!

Unapologetically,

Friday

The Real Friday Jones

REBUILDING A NEW YOU

The road ahead has promise and she can feel it.

The Real Friday Jones

PART 1

ACCOUNTING

Posted on September 13, 2012

" You're in a phase where you are required to slowly re-design, or create that aspect of yourself that you know to be true. Who are you spiritually, and what do you believe? Who are you as a person and how do you present that in your daily life? What are you interested in career wise and how are you manifesting that creative side? Do a T-chart and just start listing the good, bad and ugly about what you know to be true about you. Fix the things that you don't like and celebrate, and be that which you embrace. Design and define "WHO you are." Own and accept it.

Being that I am an accountant, I understand clearly what a T-chart is. On the left side are all of your debits – the positives, and on the right side there are all of your credits – the negatives. On a balance sheet, the idea is that you will have more positives (assets) than negatives (liabilities). But if by chance you have more negatives – it simply means you have more work to do on yourself. Taking a basic accounting of all of your positives and negatives, is one of the simplest and most revealing exercises to help you to start identifying who you are.

Below, this is what my T-chart looked like:

POSITIVES	NEGATIVES
Believe in awesomeness of God	Lack Faith sometimes.
Wake up thankful for life daily.	Uptight
Pray for loved ones daily.	Over worked.
I love.	Procrastinate sometimes.
I give.	Give too much at times.
I want to save the world.	High expectations.
Love kids.	Demanding.
Love Art.	Hard on myself.
Love Love.	Not selfish enough at times.
Love to Laugh.	Over- plan sometimes.
Love nature.	Wear my heart on my sleeve.
Give good advice.	Too Independent.
Good Friend.	Don't know how to ask for help.
I am a leader.	Too trusting.
I have a voice.	Filter too much.
I am ambitious.	Can be guarded.
I am successful.	Fret and Worry.
Love to cook.	Can be overly emotional.

Love good food.	If I get on one – I stay too long.
Love to dance.	Could have better eating habits.
Love music.	
Love my family.	
Easy going.	
Flexible.	
Aim high.	
Detailed.	
Good Planner.	
Independent.	
Super Smart.	
Trusting.	
Super Creative.	
Ideas person.	
Highly analytical.	
Love travel.	
Love to write.	
Believe in dreams.	
Sensitive	

Considerate of others.	
Protective.	
Enjoy quiet.	
Try to see the good in people.	
I acknowledge people.	
Learning not to stress.	
I am evolving.	
I am hopeful.	
I am honest.	
I keep do. I strive.	
Finding my joys.	

The process of decoding yourself, understanding your flaws, and taking an accounting so you can focus on who you really are and who you want to be is something everyone should do. I wish I had done this sooner, but at this time all things fell into place. The Therapist, The Actor, and even my brother, seemed to be in my life at the same time allowing for revealing, in-depth conversations. As human beings we have to be tuned into ourselves enough to know when change is occurring. The other day I was thinking I need a vacation of some kind. Then I thought about my last vacation. I took three bottles of wine, one for each day that I was away. And I drank all three bottles of wine by myself, and was quite tipsy, I would go as far as to say I was numb even, and I wanted to be. I am at a place where I do not want to numb myself and hide from reality. I want to explore my thoughts and further define my passions. Rather than taking down time to hide, I want to be still and listen, I want to get to know me a little better. I might even paint my body from head to toe and take pictures just to see what that might feel like and what I might look like. It sounds a little odd – but it is nothing more than a life experience and that is what we are here to do – to experience life, particularly in joyful ways. Knowing that and getting to this place is satisfying to my very soul.

Unapologetically,

Friday

PART 2

PRACTICE

Posted on September 20, 2012

"Regarding the Negative side of the T. How can you reframe you're "I" statements to be more uplifting? Example:

Lack faith sometimes. – "My faith sometimes challenges me to reach a higher level of commitment and awareness. I welcome the faith challenge."

Now try to rewrite each negative statement, and practice speaking a new language. "It's all about what we speak out of our mouth that will help our faith and beliefs."

Practice – this is such a crucial part of the process. Practice is where you actually put in work. Practice is what makes champions. I have to admit when I send my entries to The Therapist, she always adds pearls of wisdom. I never quite know what her response will be, but I am always in a little awe of how she gets me to think a little deeper – to push my growth just a little further. And I will indeed rewrite each negative statement with a more positive spin, to continue building my faith, to help me believe…

My faith at times forces me to dig deeper, practice patience, and allow for the universe to show me a different way. I am learning to appreciate exercising this muscle – with both thought and words.

Therapist Affirmation: *"My faith grows every day and I look forward to each way I can test it."*

Being uptight actually reminds me to laugh, particularly at myself. Being uptight reminds me to not take myself or my circumstances too seriously, as I am no more important to the universe than a simple grain of sand and we both are equally important.

Therapist Affirmation: *"When I'm uptight it's a reminder that I can give myself the gift of reducing the significance and allow the natural process to unfold its course."*

What is the positive spin on being overworked…? hmmm. I left a good paying job to start defining my dream life – all I can say here is my work efforts reflect the kind of life I want to have – I hope like a canvas with the first specs of paint, over time a new picture will come into view.

Therapist Affirmation: *"When I'm overworked, I remind myself that I'm more than enough, and I become more kind to myself."*

Procrastination is a reminder of how amazing I actually can be when I focus. Procrastination is an opportunity to focus. I welcome the outcomes of being focused.

Therapist Affirmation: *"Procrastination allows me to seek more creative and acceptable solutions."*

When I give too much it is an indicator that I must remember me. I have been many things to and for many people. Without help a lot of the time when help should have come from people that refused to be as responsible as me; and with help at other times, coming from loved ones at the most unexpected times and places – but now as I continue to give, I must remember me at the beginning – before I have reached the point of having nothing left to give.

Therapist Affirmation: *"When I give too much, I remind myself that I'm more than enough, and I become more kind to myself."*

High expectations mean others view me as successful – I should continue to set my expectations high, but remember to enjoy the ride.

Therapist Affirmation: *"High expectations allow me to seek and reach for the development of a better me."*

Demanding – I have to thank the Therapist for this reality check. We were talking once and she flat out asked me something along the lines of 'if you are super smart, with a creative and analytical brain equally shared, and most people are either creative (right brain) or analytical (left brain) don't you think you need to give other people time?' Ah ha. When I am being demanding I have to remember to see other people where they are and not where I want them to be.

Affirmation: *When I am being demanding I have to remember to see other people where they are and not where I want them to be.*

Being hard on myself is a learned behavior. When I start to be hard because something did not go how I wanted it to go, or a situation did not work out how I hoped, I have to remember this is life. Rules are not hardcoded; and when I want to sulk like a big kid, I have to remember I am human; and when I have done all that I can do, or what I know how to do, my actions were sufficient... as am I.

Therapist Affirmation: *"I am wonderfully and sufficiently made."*

Not selfish enough at times. The positive spin here is the same as "giving too much." I welcome the opportunity to consider the self and to consider me.

Therapist Affirmation: *"I matter."*

Planning is an opportunity to plan the details and to remember to leave space for the unexpected. An opportunity to embrace the unknown and to find comfort in not knowing.

Therapist Affirmation: *"I welcome the opportunity to plan and create future visions."*

I wear my heart on my sleeve because I choose to love. That is my choice and how others may respond is their choice. My loving, as

I do, is an opportunity for me to express without expectation. The choice to love or not is mine.

Therapist Affirmation: *"The greatest love is the love of self. It's a gift that I gladly project to others."*

My independence challenges me to be inclusive. Interdependence is as important as independence.

Therapist Affirmation: *"My independence builds self-confidence, when not used as a defensive measure."*

Trust is initially created by bonding or feeling a sense of confidence in someone. When I feel this sensation of accepting folks at face value of trusting they are as they represent themselves to be, it is important that I question and observe. Time allows people to reveal. I have to trust that time is on my side and remember to question and observe. Trusting or not trusting of anyone or any situation is also my choice.

Therapist Affirmation: *"My trust is earned. I can bank on that!"*

Filtering is consistent with thinking of others first – when I feel that I want to filter, it is an opportunity to speak in my authentic voice – to say what I want to say – unapologetically.

Affirmation: *I will assert my emotional well-being and always speak in my authentic voice."*

Being guarded, fret and worry are fear-based emotions – and each is an opportunity to grow my faith – one of my favorite bible verses is "there is no fear in love." If I am being guarded, fretting or worrying, I face my challenge to let go of fear and explore the opportunities that the unknown may present. I still myself and become available for possibility.

Therapist Affirmation: *"I walk in the endless realm of faith, for anything else inhibits my growth."*

Emotional me – whew.... When I am emotional, it is time to hit the button and stop and experience breath, stillness and going internally. Depending on the emotion, it may also be a time to breathe, find friends and be social. Either way, when I am emotional it is an opportunity to pause and re-establish self-control.

Therapist Affirmation: *"I center myself and breathe peace, gratitude and wholeness."*

Being "on one" is the opposite of filtering – it is when I want to drive my point home in an exponential kind of way, which may result in the need for apology. If I find myself "on one" in this instance I will consider others and filter. I will use the opportunity to use definitive words so that I express myself succinctly, thus reducing the need to be repetitive.

Affirmation: *"I trust that my words are sufficient."*

Most people could use better eating habits – as far as a negative, well it is what it is. I will have salad with my burger and fries – lol. Every negative that I listed is my personal challenge. Funny is, with this exercise the challenges do not seem as big. As I was writing I also reflected on past experiences that if I had a plan of action and was not wanting things to be satisfied immediately – my responses would have been different. The outcomes may have been the same, but how I felt would have been different. The saying, *you are the only person that you can control,* has great truth. Saying that however to a person that has not learned how to control their emotions is futile – it is the equivalent of giving a man a fish versus teaching him how to fish. We are the sum of our experiences and as I share my journey I hope that like me, you can choose and shape your life.

Go confidently in the direction of your dreams. Live the life you have imagined. --Henry David Thoreau

Unapologetically,

Friday

PART 3

THE FINAL CHAPTER

Posted on December 2, 2012

In closing, I would like to revisit "The Issues Part 4 – Understanding Your Self Concept"

"Your struggles are related to your self-concept. Understanding the core of who you are. It was never defined as a child from the primary caregivers. You didn't receive the basics that would help you to identify your purpose, that you were loved, and that you were worthy to be protected. No one came to rescue you. No one comforted you. No one validated you. You were a victim of a horrible situation. Not only in the home, but also in the school. Who could you as a child turn to for protection, guidance, support? You were a violated child who lived in a hostile environment."

The messaging that I received as a child was very damaging. The messaging was planted within me, infecting both my conscious thoughts and my self-conscious thoughts, affecting my emotional well-being and affecting choices that I have made over time, in ways that were not always to my benefit.

If I had to articulate the messaging that I did receive, it would go something like this: you are not pretty, your thoughts do not matter, you do not matter, your physical body is to be violated, you should be afraid, you are responsible for the life and death of other people and because of that you are to be abused by others, your feelings do not matter, you are responsible for other people's secrets, you are not worthy of love. As you can see, fear, worry, and anxiety were programmed into me at a very young age. And to be brutally honest, growing up in the Baptist Christian faith and the Sunni Muslim faith did not help, because a lot of the messaging at that time was - fear God, obey God, obey His laws or your very soul shall perish within the gates of hell. More negative programming that was fear-based. It has taken thirty-four years of my life to get to a point of understanding about myself to recognize and to be willing to change the damage that was done to me in my childhood.

When I was in Hawaii for my 40th birthday, I purchased a black KuKui bracelet. The bracelet has about ten beads on it. It is the kind of thing, whereas a child you would have asked the question "does he love me or does he love me not." I have found that wearing this simple bracelet gives me something to do when the negative messaging that can occur at lightning speed within my thoughts begins to spin out of control. I slip my beads off and counter the negative thoughts with either a single positive thought repeated ten times, or a series of ten different positive thoughts. This way I know I am thinking more positive thoughts than negative thoughts; and I also know that I am curbing some of my worries and anxieties. Re-framing how you think about things can be the difference between success and failure, and more importantly, the difference between happiness and sadness. Prolonged sadness can lead to depression and depression can be so very destructive to the human soul. If you tell yourself something long enough and if your thoughts repeat often enough in a negative way, you will start to believe them. And a trickle effect will be that every decision that you make will be from this negative space. If we can re-frame negative thoughts with positive ones, then over time the corresponding trickle effect will be that every decision that you start to make will be from a more positive place.

Let me give you an example:

Recently my firm's last retainer client terminated services because they were no longer in a position to afford the services. Now I knew this to be true because I provided a budget and the negative cash flow for the client monthly was the retainer that they were paying out to my firm.

Now this was a simple event, but the event had real consequences. The reality was that my business partner and I would have to give up our office space for a virtual office in order to cut overhead. It meant that I might have to start temping to supplement my income; and it meant, for the first time in months, I did not know where my next "paycheck" was coming from.

Based on my primary learned messaging, I could have internalized this event and started negative dialogue. Depressed dialogue would have gone something like – I am a hopeless failure, I cannot even keep a good client, I am not worth good clients, I will never have good clients, my business will never be a success. Or I could have had anxious dialogue with myself that would have gone something like – I do not have a retainer client now, how am I going to pay the mortgage, I am going to be homeless within a month because I do not have a retainer client. Now all of these thoughts are negative and truthfully highly unlikely. Will I have to change some things? Probably. Is temping the worse thing in the world? Not so much. Will things be permanently helpless? No. Are friends and family, knowing how hard I am working at my business, going to let me be homeless if they knew my situation? Highly unlikely. But if I go into a dark space and repeat these thoughts over and over, I would surely set myself up to fail.

Now the reality is I wanted to let this client go, because I realized I wanted to move more into a film space and producing space and my business partner and I agreed to change our business model to reflect that. So the client choosing to leave was perfect timing. My positive re-framing with my KuKui nut bracelet would go something like this: I am a good advisor; my clients value my professional opinion; my clients made the right choice and I aided their decision; other opportunities to earn money will present themselves to me; I am intelligent and highly marketable; I have always been a great provider for my family; I am resilient and flexible; all of my needs will be met; I love and support me; this too shall pass. And if the negative thoughts subsided and resurfaced, I would again pull my beads off and say ten positive things. This practice of mine is allowing me to develop new behavior patterns and it is allowing me to cope with challenges without beating myself up mentally and emotionally.

What I am sharing in this chapter is one of the biggest behavioral lessons I have learned through this process. I am not a licensed psychiatrist, but this re-framing of thoughts falls under something called "cognitive behavior therapy" or "automatic thought record." If you feel like you have negative thoughts that come faster than you know how to handle them, I encourage you to seek professional help with a licensed therapist. I would not have been able to write this blog and uncover some of my layers without the help of my therapist. She has been one of the angels in this life, helping me get to my purpose.

I think, based on my life experiences and women that may have had similar experiences, relationships are a challenge. I strongly encourage women, particularly if they learned negative messaging from an early age, to take the time to learn who you are. If that means putting a current relationship on pause – do it. If the guy loves, you he will wait for you. It is very important to become a whole being before seeking a mate. No other individual can "complete" you, you are amazingly made and you were born a whole being. If the people entrusted with raising you or life in general put you in a position where you have forgotten that, as an adult it is your responsibility to remember, to discover, to become whole again. Know your limits, be unafraid to say no, beat to your own drum and let the people that love you stay, and let the people that cannot relate, move on and move out. It is so important to know who you are, to love yourself, to acknowledge your feelings and to be confident enough to be unapologetic. Be you and be happy!

As a final thought I would like to leave you with a short list of ten things that Pastor Toure' Roberts of 1 Church International believes, that every woman should know. He had a two-part series on "The Year of the Woman." that I encourage you to look up online. I stumbled onto the videos, thanks to a Niecy Nash tweet a couple of days ago, and I felt like the messaging is so on point with this blog and with my life. I hope that the message encourages you and fills your heart with self-worth and with self-love.

1. My priority is my purpose.
2. My wholeness is my happiness.
3. I'm the biggest fan of me!
4. My "knower" [aka intuition] knows!
5. I will not shrink.
6. I do not accept what others falsely project [onto me].
7. It is OK not to be OK
8. My heart is priceless. I will care for it.

9. I expect to win the lotto of life.
10. I believe in miracles and restoration.

This will be my final posting to my blog until I have finished converting this blog into a book. My goal is to have someone like a Toure' Roberts or a Paul C. Brunson write the forward and/or epilogue. I want the epilogue to speak to men and to help them understand the hurts of women like me, and to equip men with the tools to relate to women like me. With statistics being 1 in 3 women will experience physical abuse, and 1 in 5 children will experience sexual abuse, there are a lot of women that need to heal and become whole; and once they are whole, there needs to be a level of understanding in the men that will love them.

I appreciate the friends and family that have gone with me on this journey. Your support in loving me, now that you know the real me, is priceless. I want to thank my therapist, you are an amazing woman and I appreciate all of your help. Words cannot express how thankful I am for knowing you and for the confidence you have had in me through this process.

Unapologetically,

Friday

The Real Friday Jones

ABOUT THE AUTHOR

KHANSA JONES-MUHAMMAD is "The Real Friday Jones," born and raised primarily in the "Do or Die" Bedford-Stuyvesant section of Brooklyn, New York during the crack cocaine epidemic and the birth of Hip-Hop. Hopefully her personal journey might inspire other people to embrace their truth and to fall in love with who they are. Friday Jones is the girl next door with a story to tell!

www.ingramcontent.com/pod-product-compliance
Lightning Source LLC
Chambersburg PA
CBHW071631080526
44588CB00010B/1356